Handbook of
Graphic Arts Equations

Handbook of Graphic Arts Equations

by
Manfred H. Breede

GATF*Press*
PITTSBURGH

Library of Congress Catalog Card Number: 99-64452
International Standard Book Number: 0-88362-246-7

Printed in the United States of America

GATF Catalog No. 1702

GATF*Press*
Graphic Arts Technical Foundation
200 Deer Run Road
Sewickley, PA 15143-2600
Phone: 412/741-6860
Fax: 412/741-2311
Email: info@gatf.org
Internet: http://www.gatf.org

Orders to:
GATF Orders
P.O. Box 1020
Sewickley, PA 15143-1020
Phone (U.S. and Canada only): 800/662-3916
Phone (all other countries): 412/741-5733
Fax: 412/741-0609
Email: gatforders@abdintl.com

GATF*Press* books are widely used by companies, associations, and schools
for training, marketing, and resale. Quantity discounts are available
by contacting Peter Oresick at 800/910-GATF.

Contents

Preface

Cannons built in 1600 could shoot as far as cannons in 1850, yet the latter cannons were much more accurate and effective weapons than their earlier counterparts. The superiority of 1850s cannons can be explained by improved military tactics and organization, improvements to limbers or ammunition chests, and greater application of scientific principles such as trajectory, projectile flight, and air resistance.

The similarities of this historical military example and the development of lithography are striking. About 100 years after the invention of lithography in 1798 by Alois Senefelder, production speeds of offset presses were about 4,000 sheets per hour. Today, top production speeds of multicolor sheetfed presses have quadrupled to about 16,000 sheets per hour and productivity as a function of the output of the entire process has increased many times more than the speed of presses alone might suggest.

Similar to the improvements made to cannons many hundreds of years ago, the productivity increases in offset lithographic printing came about by the application of new engineering, organizational, and scientific principle, without substantial changes to the offset lithographic principle itself.

Advances in engineering, metallurgical, and material sciences resulted in harder and more durable metals, helical gears, better feeders, convertible perfectors, brushless electric motors, waterless plates, to mention a few. New organizational principles such as "just-in-time delivery," standardized quality levels, and aimpoints have increased efficiency and product quality. Without new scientific principles such as laser light and the silicon chip, imagesetters and digital prepress would not have been possible.

This book is ostensibly about the mathematical calculations performed in all sectors of the graphic communications industry. The larger purpose of the book is to advance the message that this industry is still mainly about producing products by putting ink on paper. These printed products are still very much in demand and will probably remain the communication medium of choice for a long time to come unless the quality of printed products and the efficiency of their production lags behind other media forms.

Maximum quality and efficiency are achievable when new technology, as described previously, is embraced and when using procedures that are based on mathematically definable objectives.

How This Book Is Organized

This book consists of five parts, each one of which has a number of sections. The first four parts are representative of the graphic communications sectors paper, print, type, and prepress. A fifth part deals with the general topic of common conversions.

The book does not have to be read in any particular order. Each section deals with a mathematical concept that can, for the most part, be read independent of other sections. When concepts are mentioned for which more elucidating information is available elsewhere in the book, bracketed references are made to point the reader to the appropriate section.

Sections always start off with a discussion outlining the relevancy, application, and mathematical rationale of the topic at issue. Where appropriate, industry standards, important numeric information, graphics, and visual examples are presented in table, graph, and figure format.

The arithmetical portion of a section always starts with a formal mathematical representation. For greater clarity, expressions are for the most part written in meaningful terms or phrases instead of symbols. Every section is concluded with at least one "real life" example, in which the problem is stated in the narrative, followed by step-by-step calculations of all operations in their proper order.

ABACUS, contained on the appended software, can be used to verify each manually performed calculation. ABACUS and the book have the same coding system. The book parts are coded from numbers 1–5 and their respective sections are coded starting from number 1. For example, if density calculations had to be verified using the computer program, the reader would look up the book part and section numbers for density, which are 2 and 7, respectively. The computer function for density would then be found at main menu item 2 and section item 7.

To my sons Joachim and Kurt, my daughter Inga, and my wife Rosie for their encouragement and help, this book is dedicated with love.

Acknowledgments

This book was written during a sabbatical leave from my teaching duties at Ryerson Polytechnic University. I would like to thank the following people for making this sabbatical leave possible: Mary Black for recommending my proposal; Dr. Ira Levine for approving my application; Professor Rye Goodyear for help and suggestions regarding prepress; and Gillian Mothersill for assistance with typography. I also owe a debt of gratitude to Denis Coskun, friend and computer guru, on whom I could always count to bounce off new ideas. Additionally, a big thanks goes to Dr. Daniel G. Wilson for reviewing the entire book and making several excellent content suggestions, which resulted in a more comprehensive text.

Without the dynamic leadership of the Graphic Arts Technical Foundation, technical writers like myself would not be able to reach a wide international readership and much gratitude is due to the following people at this remarkable organization: Peter M. Oresick for giving me the privilege of authoring this book; Amy Woodall for her courteous efficiency and prompt attention to my queries; Tom Destree for redrawing most of my original line drawings, rendering the book clearer and more attractive; and finally, Tamara Moore for crafting my manuscript into the readable book I hoped it would become.

Part 1
Paper

The breathtaking rate of progress in computer technology that permits storage and retrieval of information in digital format instead of paper has given rise in recent years to predictions of a greatly reduced demand for paper. Some even proclaim a future paperless society, but to paraphrase Mark Twain's repudiation of his own demise, "The death of paper has been greatly exaggerated."

In fact, if recent worldwide paper consumption statistics are an indication of what the future holds, the use of paper is on a steady increase, so much so that the concerns are not with the demand for paper but the economic availability of it.

It is an undeniable fact that integrated digital media elements, or multimedia, have the theoretical potential of replacing paper because, just like images printed on paper, they accomplish the fundamental function of rendering text and graphic images visible to a reader. Moreover, multimedia has the distinct advantage of incorporating, in addition to text and still images, sound and animation.

These new media advantages beg the question: Why do images printed on paper, in spite of their inherent limitations, show no signs of abating in popularity? The answer to this question is complex and probably related to man's cultural conditioning, which could change with the passage of time. This means that no one, least of all self-appointed technological prophets, can predict the future with certainty.

There is, however, an economic constant that has always been instrumental in a technology's success or failure. History is full of precedents in which the economic benefits of new technology were so obvious that it was adopted universally in relatively short order.

The invention of movable type by Gutenberg was one such historical precedent. Books produced by movable type were at the time considered to be of inferior quality compared to the then-common hand-scripted books. Yet movable type resulted in such enormous productivity advantages that books produced using this revolutionary technology became the new standard everywhere.

It is in this spirit that the following thirteen sections on paper were written, because the economic use and purchase of paper is a key factor in the print media's ability to compete successfully with alternate paperless forms of communication.

1 Basis Weight and Grammage

Notwithstanding paper's relative fragility, increasing its raw material concentrations gives it more substance and effectively increases its weight per unit area. Papermakers manufacture a wide variety of papers with different weights to satisfy printers' economic prerogatives or quality requirements.

The cost of paper is, to a large degree, dependent on its substance concentrations and increases at about the same rate as its weight. For example, newspaper publishers often look at ways to reduce their manufacturing costs by using lighter grades of newsprint, while maintaining necessary quality standards such as opacity for readability and stiffness for handling.

Heavier paper is a quality requirement for less utilitarian products, such as illustrated books, because heavier paper is more opaque due to its increased thickness, thus reducing undesirable showthrough.

Lighter and consequently thinner papers are necessary for products such as voluminous religious texts or reference literature in order to keep the physical size of books to more user-friendly proportions.

All other things being equal, the cost of paper is ultimately related to its weight; hence, anyone professionally engaged in its purchase would do well to gain a thorough understanding of the two paper weight measures, grammage and basis weight.

Grammage is the less complex of the two systems and can be defined as the weight in grams of a single sheet of paper having an area of one square meter.

Unlike basis weight, grammage values are always directly comparable with values of papers that belong to different classifications because grammage is based universally on the same unit area of 1 m^2. More specifically, this means that, regardless of papers being bond, book, or cover, their grammage values can be used to rank them according to their weight. This may be the single most important advantage of grammage over its counterpart, basis weight.

Grammage is the standard unit of measurement for paper weight specification in most European countries and is increasingly being adopted in North America.

While grammage is based on the metric units gram and meter, basis weight uses the imperial units inch and pound.

A basis weight value pertains only to a particular paper classification. Each paper classification has a different unit area, called its basic size, on which its basis weight is founded. Owing to this fact, absolute weight comparisons between papers from different classifications cannot be made with basis weights without further calculations.

Basis weight is the weight in pounds of a ream of paper (500 sheets) having a designated unit area in inches that is unique for a specific paper classification.

Table 1.1.1.
Basic sizes in inches and square areas for paper classifications.

Bond, ledger, writing, onionskin
17×22 = 374 sq. in.

Bristol
$22\frac{1}{2} \times 28\frac{1}{2}$ = 641.25 sq. in.

Cover
20×26 = 520 sq. in.

Kraft, newsprint, tag
24×36 = 864 sq. in.

Index
$25\frac{1}{2} \times 30\frac{1}{2}$ = 777.75 sq. in.

Uncoated book, coated book, C1S label, C2S offset, offset
25×38 = 950 sq. in.

Printing bristol
$22\frac{1}{2} \times 35$ = 787.5 sq. in.

Blank
22×28 = 616 sq. in.

To state a basis weight in a meaningful way, it is necessary to know its corresponding paper classification. Otherwise, an 80-lb. basis weight, for example, could be interpreted to mean either 80-lb. book or 80-lb. cover paper. The real weight for a cover paper interpretation would be much higher than for a book paper interpretation by virtue of a cover paper's much smaller basic size.

The following tables show paper weights for five paper classifications. The basis weight range for each paper classification appears in the top row. Underneath each basis weight are columns of weights per 1,000 sheets for various standard sizes, which are also known as M weights.

These weights are nominal and could vary as much as ±5% from their nominal values. For example, the acceptable range for an 80-lb. paper would be between 76 and 84 lb. The term substance is sometimes used for bond, ledger, safety, writing, and onionskin papers instead of basis weight.

Tables 1.1.2–1.1.6 are interpreted with basis weights listed at the heads of each column and the M weights below them. The standard sizes available for each paper classification are listed in the first column. Note that the standard size that corresponds with the basic size of its paper classification always has an M weight equal to twice its basis weight. For example, consider Table 1.1.4, row 7, standard size 25×38.

Table 1.1.2.
Standard weights of tag papers.

Weights per 1,000 sheets
Basis 24×36

			Basis and M Weights*				
Size	**90**	**100**	**125**	**150**	**175**	**200**	**250**
22½×28½	134	148	186	223	260	297	371
24×36	180	200	250	300	350	400	500
28½×45	268	296	372	446	520	594	742

*Basis weights in bold.

Basis Weight to Grammage Conversion Equation 1

$$\text{Basis weight to grammage} = \frac{\text{Basis weight} \times 703{,}700}{\text{Area of basic size} \times 500}$$

where 703,700 is a constant factor and the area of basic size is given in Table 1.1.1.

Table 1.1.3.
Standard weights
of bond, ledger, safety,
writing, and onionskin
papers.

Weights per 1,000 sheets
Basis 17×22

Substance and M Weights*

Size	9	13	16	20	24	28	32	36	40	44
8½×11	4.5	6.5	8	10	12	14	16	18	20	22
8½×13	5.32	7.68	9.44	11.81	14.18	16.54	18.90	21.27	23.63	26
8½×14	5.73	8.26	10.18	12.72	15.26	17.81	20.36	22.90	25.45	28
11×17	9	13	16	20	24	28	32	36	40	44
16×21	16	23½	29	36	43	50½	57½	65	72	79
16×42	32½	47	58	72	86	101	115	130	144	158
17×22	18	26	32	40	48	56	64	72	80	88
17½×22½	19	27	34	42	51	59	67	76	84	93
17×26	21½	31	38	47	57	66	76	85	95	104
17×28	23	33	41	51	61	71½	81½	92	102	112
18×23	20	29	35½	44½	53	62	71	80	89	97½
18×46	40	58	71	89	106	124	142	160	178	195
19×24	22	32	39	49	58½	68½	78	88	98	107
20×28	27	39	48	60	72	84	96	108	120	132
20×32	31	47	58	72	86	101	115	130	144	158
22×25½	27	39	48	60	62	84	96	108	120	132
22×34	36	52	64	80	96	112	128	144	160	176
22½×22½	25	35	43	54	65	76	87	97	108	119
22½×34½	37½	54	66	83	99	116	133	149	166	183
22½×35	38	56	67	84	101	118	134	152	168	186
23×36	40	58	71	89	106	124	142	160	178	195
24×38	44	64	78	98	117	137	156	176	196	214
24½×24½	29	42	51½	64	77	90	103	116	128½	141
24½×28½	33½	49	60	75	90	105	119½	134½	149½	164½
24½×29	34	49½	61	76	91	106½	122	137	152	167
24½×38½	46	66	81	101	121	141½	161½	182	202	222
24½×39	46	66	82	102	122	144	164	184	204	225
25½×44	54	78	96	120	144	168	192	216	240	264
26×34	42½	62	76	94	114	132	152	170	189	208
28×34	46	66	82	102	122	143	163	184	204	224
34×44	72	104	128	160	192	224	256	288	320	352
35×45	76	109	135	168	202	236	270	303	337	371

*Basis weights in bold.
Because of the greater accuracy required when multiplying M weights for smaller sizes, rows 1–3 use decimal values.

Table 1.1.4. Standard weights of uncoated book, coated book, C1S label, C2S offset, and offset papers.

Weights per 1,000 Sheets
Basis 25×38

						Basis and M Weights*						
Size	**30**	**35**	**40**	**45**	**50**	**60**	**70**	**80**	**90**	**100**	**120**	**150**
17½×22½	25	29	33	37	41	50	58	66	75	83	99	124
19×25	30	35	40	45	50	60	70	80	90	100	120	150
23×29	42	49	56	63	70	84	98	112	126	140	169	
23×35	51	59	68	76	85	102	119	136	152	170	204	
22½×35	50	58	66	75	83	99	116	133	149	166	199	249
24×36	54	64	72	82	90	110	128	146	164	182	218	272
25×38	60	70	80	90	100	120	140	160	180	200	240	300
26×40	66	76	88	98	110	132	154	176	198	218	262	328
28×42	74	86	100	112	124	148	174	198	222	248	298	372
28×44	78	90	104	116	130	156	182	208	234	260	312	390
30½×41	78	92	106	118	132	158	184	210	236	264	316	396
32×44	88	104	118	134	148	178	208	238	266	296	356	444
33×44	92	106	122	138	152	184	214	244	276	306	366	460
35×45	100	116	132	150	166	198	232	266	298	332	398	498
36×48	108	128	144	164	180	220	254	292	328	364	436	544
38×50	120	140	160	180	200	240	280	320	360	400	480	600
41×54	140	164	186	210	234	280	326	372	420	466	560	700
44×64	178	208	238	266	296	356	414	474	534	592	712	888
35×46	102	118	136	152	170	204	238	272	306	338	406	
38×52	124	146	166	188	208	250	292	332	374	416	500	
41×61	156	184	212	236	264	316	368	420	472	528	632	
42×58	154	180	206	230	256	308	358	510	462	512	615	
44×66	178	208	238	266	296	356	414	474	534	592	712	
46×69	201	234	267	301	334	400	468	534	602	668	802	
52×76	250	292	332	374	416	500	582	666	748	832	998	

*Basis weights in bold.

*Basis weights in bold.

Table 1.1.5.
Standard weights of
cover papers.

Weights per 1,000 sheets
Basis 20×26

	Basis and M Weights*						
Size	**50**	**60**	**65**	**80**	**90**	**100**	**130**
20×26	100	120	130	160	180	200	260
22½×28½	123	148	160	197	222	246	320
23×29	128	154	167	205	231	256	334
23×35	155	186	201	248	279	310	402
26×40	200	240	260	320	360	400	520
35×46	310	372	402	496	558	620	804

*Basis weights in bold.

Table 1.1.6.
Standard weights of
index papers.

Weights per 1,000 sheets
Basis 25½×30½

	Basis and M Weights*				
Size	**90**	**110**	**140**	**170**	**220**
20½×24½	116¼	142	180¾	219½	284¾
22½×28½	148½	181½	230¾	280¼	362¾
22½×35	182¼	222¾	283½	344¼	445½
25½×30½	180	220	280	340	440
28½×45	296¾	362¾	461¾	560¾	725½

*Basis weights in bold.

Example

If a bond paper has a basis weight of 24 lb., then:

$$\text{Grammage} = \frac{24 \times 703,700}{374 \times 500}$$

$$= \frac{16,888,800}{187,000}$$

$$= 90.3144385$$

$$\approx 90 \text{ g/m}^2$$

**Basis Weight
to Grammage
Conversion
Equation 2**

$$\text{Grammage} = \frac{\text{Basis weight} \times 1,407.4}{\text{Area of basic size}}$$

where 1,407.4 is a constant factor and the area of basic size
is given in Table 1.1.1.

Example

If a bond paper has a basis weight of 24 lb., then:

$$\text{Grammage} = \frac{24 \times 1{,}407.4}{374}$$

$$= \frac{33{,}777.6}{374}$$

$$= 90.3144385$$

$$\approx 90 \text{ g/m}^2$$

Note the identical results of equations 1 and 2.

Grammage to Basis Weight Conversion Equation 1

$$\text{Basis weight} = \frac{\text{Area of basic size} \times 500 \times \text{Grammage}}{703{,}700}$$

where 703,700 is a constant factor and the area of basic size is given in Table 1.1.1.

Example

If an offset paper has a grammage of 89 g/m², then:

$$\text{Basis weight} = \frac{950 \times 500 \times 89}{703{,}700}$$

$$= \frac{42{,}275{,}000}{703{,}700}$$

$$= 60.07531619$$

$$\approx 60\text{-lb. basis weight}$$

Grammage to Basis Weight Conversion Equation 2

$$\text{Basis weight} = \frac{\text{Area of basic size} \times \text{Grammage}}{1{,}407.4}$$

where 1,407.4 is a constant factor and the area of basic size is given in Table 1.1.1.

Example

If an offset paper has a grammage of 89 g/m², then:

$$\text{Basis weight} = \frac{950 \times 89}{1{,}407.4}$$

$$= \frac{84{,}550}{1{,}407.4}$$

$$= 60.07531619$$

$$\approx 60\text{-lb. basis weight}$$

Note the identical results of equations 1 and 2.

2 M Weight

To the extent that papermakers package their product mostly in increments of 1,000 sheets and price it according to weight, specifying paper quantities by the weight of 1,000 sheets, or M weight, is advantageous.

The definition of M weight is the weight in pounds of 1,000 sheets of paper of a given size specified in inches.

Most paper price lists and catalogs indicate M weights and their corresponding paper sizes in columnar form, as seen in Tables 1.1.2–1.1.6 in the previous section. The M weights included herein are derived from the same mathematical method discussed in this section.

By convention, M weights are stated as follows:

$$35{\times}45{-}168M$$

where 35×45 is the paper size in inches and 168M is the weight in pounds for 1,000 sheets.

If the M weight of a paper is stated without dimensions, such as Victoria bond 48M, it is assumed to be a bond paper's M weight in its basic size.

Labels affixed to paper packaging will invariably also show its M weight. M weight alone, however, is no affirmation of its basis weight. Without further calculations we cannot be sure, for example, of the basis weight of an M weight 35×45–168M. Before any calculations can begin, it is also necessary to know the paper's classification because the conversion equation requires the paper's basic size area.

Once basis weights of papers are known, absolute weight comparisons can be made, albeit exclusively for papers belonging to the same classification.

M Weight to Basis Weight Equation

$$\text{Basis weight} = \frac{\text{M weight} \times \text{Area of basic size}}{\text{Area of M weight paper} \times 2}$$

where the area of basic size is defined in Table 1.1.1.

Example

Suppose a label affixed to the packaging of a bond paper reads 35×45–168M, then:

$$\text{Basis weight} = \frac{168 \times 374}{35 \times 45 \times 2}$$

$$= 628323150$$

$$= 19.94666667$$

$$\approx 20 \text{ lb.}$$

The result can be verified in Table 1.1.3 (bond papers).

Basis Weight to M Weight Equation

$$\text{M weight} = \frac{\text{Basis weight} \times \text{Area of M weight sheet} \times 2}{\text{Area of basic size}}$$

where the area of basic size is defined in Table 1.1.1.

Example

Suppose a 90-lb. coated book paper measures 44×64 in., then:

$$\text{M weight} = \frac{90 \times 44 \times 64 \times 2}{950}$$

$$= \frac{506,880}{950}$$

$$= 533.5578947$$

$$\approx 534 \text{ lb.}$$

The result can be verified in Table 1.1.3 (coated book papers).

M Weight to Grammage Equation

$$\text{Grammage} = \frac{\text{M weight} \times 703,700}{\text{Area of M weight sheet} \times 1,000}$$

where 703,700 is a constant factor.

Example   The grammage of a 35×45–168M paper is:

$$\text{Grammage} = \frac{168 \times 703{,}700}{35 \times 45 \times 1{,}000}$$

$$= \frac{118{,}221{,}600}{1{,}575{,}000}$$

$$= 75.06133333$$

$$\approx 75 \text{ g/m}^2$$

3   Ream Weight

A ream is 500 sheets of paper, which is also the amount of paper used to calculate basis weight. Ream weight is the weight of 500 sheets of paper of any given size. If by happenstance, a paper's ream weight is measured in its basic size, then the ream weight is also the basis weight of this paper.

Other than ream weight being based on 500 sheets it is identical in all other respects to M weight. It follows that ream weight is always exactly one-half the amount of M weight.

Basis Weight to Ream Weight Equation

$$\text{Ream weight} = \frac{\text{Basis weight} \times \text{Area of M weight sheet}}{\text{Area of basic size}}$$

where the area of basic size is given in Table 1.1.1.

Example

Suppose a 90-lb. coated book paper measures 44×64 in., then:

$$\text{Ream weight} = \frac{90 \times 44 \times 64}{950}$$

$$= \frac{253,440}{950}$$

$$= 266.7789474$$

$$\approx 267 \text{ lb.}$$

The result can be verified in Table 1.1.4 (offset papers). Ream weight is one-half of M weight.

4   Equivalent Weights of Paper

Since absolute weights of two papers from different classifications are not comparable due to their dissimilar weight-to-area ratios, a method that effectively calculates the weight of both papers based on a common weight-to-area ratio has to be completed. This is commonly known as equivalent weight of papers. Tables that are based on this mathematical method can also be used to determine equivalent weights for the various paper classifications (Table 1.4.1).

A specific application for this function would be an instance where a bond paper had to be found that equals the weight of a 50-lb. book paper. The procedure involves the conversion of a book paper's basis weight derived from a 25×38-in. basic size area to what the same book paper would weigh in bond paper's basic size area of 17×22 in. The result gives the equivalent weight of a bond paper that matches a book paper in weight.

Equivalent Weight of Paper Equation

$$EWP = \frac{\text{Basic size of equivalent sheet} \times \text{Basis weight of sheet to be exchanged}}{\text{Area of basic size of sheet to be exchanged}}$$

where the area of basic size is given in Table 1.1.1.

Example

Suppose a 50-lb. book paper had to be exchanged with a bond paper of equal weight, then:

$$EWP = \frac{374 \times 50}{950}$$

$$= \frac{18{,}700}{950}$$

Table 1.4.1.
Equivalent weights
of paper.

	Bond 17×22	Book 25×38	Cover 20×26	Vellum 22½×28½	Printing 22½×35	Index 25½×30½	Tag 24×36
Bond,	13	33	18	22	27	27	30
Ledger,	16	41	22	27	34	33	37
Writing	20	51	28	34	42	42	46
	24	61	33	41	51	50	56
	28	71	39	48	59	58	64
	32	81	45	55	67	67	74
	36	91	50	62	76	75	83
	40	102	56	69	84	83	93
	44	112	61	75	93	92	102
Uncoated	12	30	16	20	25	25	27
Book, Coated	16	40	21	27	33	32	36
Book, C1S	18	45	24	30	37	37	41
Label, C2S	20	50	27	34	41	41	45
Offset, Offset	24	60	32	40	50	49	55
	28	70	38	47	58	57	64
	31	80	43	54	66	66	73
	35	90	48	60	75	74	82
	39	100	54	67	83	81	91
	47	120	65	80	99	98	109
	59	150	80	100	124	123	136
Cover	29	73	40	49	61	60	66
	36	91	50	62	76	75	82
	43	110	60	74	91	90	100
	47	119	65	80	98	97	108
	58	146	80	99	121	120	134
	65	164	90	111	136	135	149
	72	183	100	124	151	150	166
Vellum	58	148	81	100	123	121	135
or Mill	70	176	97	120	147	146	162
Bristol	82	207	114	140	172	170	189
	93	237	130	160	196	194	216
	105	267	146	180	221	218	242
	117	296	162	200	246	243	269
Printing	52	133	73	90	110	109	121
Bristol	59	151	83	102	125	123	137
	71	181	99	122	150	148	165
	83	211	116	143	175	173	192
	95	241	132	163	200	198	219
Index	43	110	60	74	91	90	100
	53	135	74	91	112	110	122
	67	170	93	115	141	140	156
	82	208	114	140	172	170	189
	105	267	146	182	223	220	244
Tag	43	110	60	74	91	90	100
	54	137	75	93	114	113	125
	65	165	90	111	137	135	150
	76	192	105	130	160	158	175
	87	220	120	148	183	180	200
	109	275	151	186	228	225	250
	130	330	181	222	273	270	300

$$= 19.68421053$$

$$\approx 20$$

Therefore, 20-lb. bond paper is equivalent to 50-lb. book paper. The result can be verified in Table 1.4.1.

5   Hundred Weight (CWT)

The sum total of a paper's value is intrinsically related to the complexity of its manufacturing process, the type of raw material, and the amount or concentration of raw materials contained in the paper. The paper classification and grade of paper is largely dependent on complexity and raw material types, while raw material concentration determines its basis weight. An objective price analysis can only be made when papers of like classification, grade, and basis weight are compared.

Hundred weight or CWT is a term that simply means the price of paper per 100 lb., and as such is an excellent pricing unit to make objective price comparisons provided the afore-mentioned conditions are met.

To calculate CWT, the price of paper per given M weight must be obtained from a price list such as that shown in Table 1.5.1. Dividing the price of 1,000 sheets by its own M weight gives the price of the paper per pound, and multiply-ing it by 100 yields the price of the paper for 100 lb. or its CWT.

The decision as to which among a group of papers that are identical in all respects other than their hundred weight should be purchased can now be made on the basis of the lowest CWT.

From Table 1.5.1 it is apparent that price differentials exist even within a paper classification. The most obvious price differential is based on the concept of volume discount, i.e., increasing quantities purchased reduces the price of paper considerably. To illustrate this concept further, Table 1.5.1 shows a CWT differential of $22 between the purchase of one carton and eight cartons of 25×38–90M paper.

The other less obvious price differential is based on basis weight. Lighter papers have higher CWTs by reason of

Table 1.5.1.
Sample paper price list.

Concorde Offset Vellum Finish Blue-White		1 Carton or 125 lb. Assorted	4 Cartons or 500 lb. Assorted	8 Cartons or 1,000 lb. Assorted
			Price per 100 lb.	
	Basis 25×38–90M	132.50	115.00	110.50
	Basis 25×38–110M	131.00	113.50	109.00
	Basis 25×38–130M	130.00	112.50	108.00
Basic Size 25×38	Sheets per Carton		Price per 1,000 Sheets	
90M				
17½×22½–37M	3,000	49.03	42.55	40.89
19×25–45M	3,000	59.63	51.75	49.73
23×35–76M	1,500	100.70	87.40	83.98
25×38–90M	1,500	119.25	103.50	99.45
28×40–106M	1,000	140.45	121.90	117.13
35×45–149M	1,000	197.43	171.35	164.65
110M				
17½×22½–46M	3,000	60.26	52.21	50.14
19×25–55M	2,000	72.05	62.43	59.95
23×35–93M	1,500	121.83	105.56	101.37
25×38–110M	1,250	144.10	124.85	119.90
28×40–130M	1,000	170.30	147.55	141.70
35×45–182M	750	238.42	206.57	198.38
130M				
17½×22½–54M	2,000	70.20	60.75	58.32
19×25–65M	2,000	84.50	73.13	70.20
23×35–110M	1,000	143.00	123.75	118.80
25×38–130M	1,000	169.00	146.25	140.40
28×40–153M	750	198.90	172.13	165.24
35×45–215M	500	279.50	241.88	232.20

higher production costs associated with lighter-weight papers. This again can be seen in Table 1.5.1, where the CWTs for 25×38–90M and the heavier 25×38–130M are $132.50 and $130, respectively.

CWT Equation

$$CWT = \frac{\text{Price per M weight sheets} \times 100}{\text{M weight}}$$

Example 1   If the price for one carton of Concorde offset paper 23×35–110M is listed as $143, then:

$$\text{CWT} = \frac{143 \times 100}{110}$$

$$= \frac{14{,}300}{110}$$

$$= \$130$$

Example 2   If the price for one carton of Concorde offset paper 19×25–45M is listed as $59.63, then:

$$\text{CWT} = \frac{59.63 \times 100}{45}$$

$$= \frac{5963}{45}$$

$$= 132.51111$$

$$\approx \$132.50$$

The results can be verified in Table 1.5.1. Note that the heavier 130M paper has a lower CWT than the lighter 90M paper.

6   The Price of Paper

**How Is the
Price of Paper
Calculated
Using a
Paper Price
Catalog?**

Graphic communications' distinguishing characteristic, as opposed to other communications industries, is its dependence on imaged substrates to dispatch information. Although not exclusively so, the most common substrate used in the printing industry is paper. The economic availability and use of paper therefore has a major impact on the price of printed products. In fact, the cost of paper can be the determining factor in whether printing products are an economically viable alternative to other modes of communication.

The causation of economic availability is, for the most part, beyond the reach of most printers, but the economic use of paper is well within their control and begins with purchasing the right classification, grade, size, and weight of paper at the lowest possible price.

Paper price catalogs must be fully understood in that they provide information for potential paper cost savings by way of volume discount or paper weight reductions.

Save for minor details, paper price catalogs are issued in a standard format of which Table 1.5.1 is a typical example. It shows the available range of prices per 1,000 sheets for one paper grade and classification—in this case an offset paper with the trade name Concorde, which is sold in 90M, 110M, and 130M weights. (For further information on M weight, refer to section 2.)

The standard sizes available for Concorde offset are listed at the beginning of each row, followed by the number of sheets packaged per carton. The number of sheets per carton tends to be lower with larger standard sizes in order to reduce the weight per carton for easier handling of the cartons.

Although paper can be purchased in any special size, it is almost always more economical to go with a standard size, even if the standard size is somewhat larger than the special size. The exception is large orders that require certain minimum quantities for special sizes that depend on the width and production speed of the paper machine, with wider and faster paper machines requiring larger minimum orders than narrower and slower paper machines.

Table 1.5.1 shows the price structure for three quantities ranging from one to eight cartons. This is listed in three columns using two pricing units, the price per 100 lb. or CWT (see section 5), and the price per M sheets or 1,000 sheets.

Table 1.5.1 shows that the price differential between one- and eight-carton orders can be as much as $47.30 for a 35×45–215M paper for every 1,000 sheets ordered (last row in the table).

Even greater savings are possible when purchasing paper on skids, reflecting the reduced packaging cost incurred by the papermaker. Table 1.6.1 shows the price for the same name brand, Concorde offset, when purchased in standard skids.

Table 1.6.1.
Sample price list for paper purchased in standard skids.

Concorde Offset		
Vellum finish		Price per 100 lb.
Blue-white Basis 25×38–90M		95.25
Basic size 25×38	Sheets per skid	Price per 1,000 sheets
90M 28×40–106M	19,000	100.97

The hundred weight is $95.25 and the price per 28×40–106M is $100.97, which compares with the lowest hundred weight of $110.50 and price per 1,000 sheets of $117.13 for the same paper purchased in cartons. The result is further savings of $15.25 per 100 lb. or $16.16 per 1,000 sheets.

Volume discount is also offered when ordering assorted weights, such as an order that consists of 90M, 110M, and 130M papers. The determining factor in this case is not the number of cartons ordered for each individual weight category but the total weight of the combined order. The minimum quantities to qualify for assorted weight discounts are listed in Table 1.5.1 at 125, 500, and 1,000 lb.

Finally, price savings can be achieved when an interchange of a heavier paper with a lighter paper is possible without negatively affecting the printed product's quality. For instance, Table 1.5.1 lists the price for 25×38–130M paper at $169, while the lighter 25×38–90M paper sells for only $119.25; this accounts for a price differential of $49.75 per 1,000 sheets.

Once the price category has been determined, the total price of a paper order can be calculated using either the M sheets price (price per 1,000 sheets) or CWT price (price per 100 lb.). Both methods will result in identical prices. (For further information on M weight and CWT, refer to sections 2 and 5.)

Price per M Sheets Equation

$$\text{Price per M sheets} = \frac{\text{Total no. of sheets} \times \text{M sheet price}}{1,000}$$

Example 1

Suppose 100,000 sheets of 35×45–215M Concorde offset for an advertisement flyer could be substituted with a lighter 35×45–149M Concorde offset without any ill effects to the print quality; the price differential between the lighter and heavier papers is determined as shown below. According to Table 1.5.1:

Both paper weights qualify for the lowest price, as each order exceeds eight cartons.

No. of 35×45–215M sheets = 100,000

M sheet price for 35×45–215M = 232.20

$$\text{Paper price} = \frac{100,000 \times 232.20}{1,000}$$

$$= \frac{23,220,000}{1,000}$$

$$= \$23,220.00$$

No. of 35×45–149M sheets = 100,000

M sheet price for 35×45–149M = 164.65

$$\text{Paper price} = \frac{100,000 \times 164.65}{1,000}$$

$$= \frac{16,465,000}{1,000}$$

$$= \$16,465.00$$

$$\text{Price differential} = 23,220 - 16,465$$

$$= \$6,755.00$$

Example 2   If the June issue of a publication requires 8,000 sheets of 28×40–130M Concorde offset and the paper was purchased in two separate orders of 4,000 sheets, while the paper for the July issue was purchased in a single 8,000-sheet order, the paper price differential between both issues is determined as shown below. According to Table 1.5.1:

No. of sheets for June issue's first order = 4,000

M sheet price for 28×40–130M = 147.55

$$\text{Paper price} = \frac{4,000 \times 147.55}{1,000}$$

$$= \frac{590,200}{1,000}$$

$$= \$590.20$$

Since the second order for the June issue is the same in all respects to the first order, its price is identical.

Total paper price for June issue = 590.20 + 590.20

$$= \$1,180.40$$

No. of sheets for July's issue = 8,000

M sheet price = 141.70

$$\text{Paper price} = \frac{8,000 \times 141.70}{1,000}$$

$$= \frac{1,133,600}{1,000}$$

$$= \$1,133.60$$

$$\text{Price differential} = 1,180.40 - 1,133.60$$

$$= \$46.80$$

Example 3
If a presentation folder requiring 3,000 sheets of 35×45–149M paper, 3,000 sheets of 28×40–130M paper, and 3,000 sheets of 25×38–130M paper were purchased in three separate orders as opposed to a single order, the price differential is determined as shown below. According to Table 1.5.1:

Separate orders:

All three papers are purchased at the highest price because their quantities are below the minimum of four cartons per order to qualify for the next lower price category.

No. of 35×45–149M sheets = 3,000

M sheet price for 35×45–149M = 197.40

$$\text{Paper price} = \frac{3,000 \times 197.40}{1,000}$$

$$= \frac{592,200}{1,000}$$

$$= \$592.20$$

No. of 28×40–130M sheets = 3,000

M sheet price for 28×40–130M = 170.30

$$\text{Paper price} = \frac{3,000 \times 170.30}{1,000}$$

$$= \frac{510,900}{1,000}$$

$$= \$510.90$$

No. of 25×38–130M sheets = 3,000

M sheet price for 25×38–130M = 169.00

$$\text{Paper price} = \frac{3,000 \times 169}{1,000}$$

$$= \frac{507,000}{1,000}$$

$$= \$507.00$$

Total paper price = 592.20 + 510.90
+ 507.00

$$= \$1,610.10$$

Assorted order:

Weight of 3,000 sheets 35×45–149M = 3 × 149

$$= 447$$

Weight of 3,000 sheets 28×40–130M = 3 × 130

$$= 390$$

Weight of 3,000 sheets 25×38–130M = 3 × 130

$$= 390$$

Total weight = 447 + 390 + 390

$$= 1,227 \text{ lb.}$$

Since 1,227 lb. is greater than 1,000 lb., the lowest price applies.

Number of 35×45–149M sheets = 3,000

M sheet price of 35×45–149M = 164.65

$$\text{Paper price} = \frac{3{,}000 \times 164.65}{1{,}000}$$

$$= \frac{493{,}950}{1{,}000}$$

$$= \$493.95$$

Number of 28×40–130M sheets = 3,000

M sheet price of 28×40–130M = 141.70

$$\text{Paper price} = \frac{3{,}000 \times 141.70}{1{,}000}$$

$$= \frac{425{,}100}{1{,}000}$$

$$= \$425.10$$

No. of 25×38–130M sheets = 3,000

M sheet price for 25×38–130M = 140.40

$$\text{Paper price} = \frac{3{,}000 \times 140.40}{1{,}000}$$

$$= \frac{421{,}200}{1{,}000}$$

$$= \$421.20$$

Total paper price = 493.95 + 425.10
+ 421.20

$$= \$1{,}340.25$$

$$\text{Price differential} = 1{,}610.10 - 1{,}340.25$$

$$= \$269.85$$

Price per CWT Equation

$$\text{Price per CWT} = \frac{\text{Total weight in pounds} \times \text{CWT price}}{100}$$

Example 1

If the price of paper in example 3 (M sheets method, assorted order) is calculated with the price per CWT method, then:

Since the total weight of 1,227 lb. exceeds 1,000 lb., the lowest price for each weight category applies.

$$\text{CWT price for } 35{\times}45\text{–}149\text{M} = 110.50$$

$$\text{Total weight of } 35{\times}45\text{–}149\text{M} = 3 \times 149$$

$$= 447 \text{ lb.}$$

$$\text{Paper price} = \frac{447 \times 110.50}{100}$$

$$= \frac{49{,}393.500}{100}$$

$$= 493.935$$

$$\approx \$493.94$$

$$\text{CWT price for } 28{\times}40\text{–}130\text{M} = 109.00$$

$$\text{Total weight of } 28{\times}40\text{–}130\text{M} = 3 \times 130$$

$$= 390 \text{ lb.}$$

$$\text{Paper price} = 390 \times 109.00100$$

$$= 42{,}510{,}100$$

$$= \$425.10$$

$$\text{CWT price for } 25{\times}38\text{–}130\text{M} = 108.00$$

Total weight of 25×38–130M $= 3 \times 130$

$$= 390 \text{ lb.}$$

$$\text{Paper price} = \frac{390 \times 108.00}{100}$$

$$= \frac{42,120}{100}$$

$$= \$421.20$$

$$\text{Total price} = 493.94 + 425.10 + 421.20$$

$$= \$1,340.24$$

Please note that the prices of the M sheet and CWT methods are identical within one cent.

7   Bulk Determination

Unless the additive effect of many assembled sheets of paper is taken into consideration, printed products such as books could turn out to be either too thick or too thin. Printers of voluminous reading materials are particularly interested in the thickness of books or volumes of books, ensued from various paper calipers. Papermakers often provide this information for book papers used in encyclopedias, religious texts, directories, and catalogs. Table 1.7.1 lists such information for a book paper.

Table 1.7.1.
Information for determining the thickness of book paper.

Printers opaque Blue white Vellum finish Basis weights 25×38–500				
Basis Weight	**Caliper***	**Pages/Inch**	**Opacity**	**Brightness**
26	0.0090	890	82	80
28	0.0095	840	83	80
30	0.0102	780	85	80
33	0.0112	710	86	80
35	0.0120	670	88	80

*Caliper of four sheets in inches.

As might be expected, the number of pages per inch decreases as the caliper of the paper increases. Table 1.7.1 also illustrates that within a paper grade, caliper and the resulting pages per inch are a function of basis weight. As basis weight increases, the caliper also increases. It must be understood, however, that this is only true within a paper grade. It is quite possible for another paper grade to yield different calipers for the same basis weight. This is due to dissimilar raw materials and manufacturing processes entailed by various paper grades.

An undesirable consequence of reduced caliper is the simultaneous decrease of opacity. Table 1.7.1 lists opacities of 82% and 88% for 26- and 35-lb. papers, respectively. Reduced opacity causes showthrough and results in decreased legibility of two-sided printed products such as books. It can thus be seen that a requirement for thin paper must be moderated by the need for a minimum of opacity.

Table 1.7.2 shows a range of typical printing papers' caliper and page-per-inch relationships. It is based on the mathematical method discussed in this section. The micrometer readings were derived from the aggregate thick-

Table 1.7.2.
Paper caliper and pages per inch.

Micrometer Reading	Pages per Inch	Micrometer Reading	Pages per Inch	Micrometer Reading	Pages per Inch
0.007	1,143	0.019	421	0.031	258
0.0075	1,067	0.0195	410	0.0315	254
0.008	1,000	0.020	400	0.032	250
0.0085	941	0.0205	390	0.0325	246
0.009	889	0.021	381	0.033	242
0.0095	842	0.0215	372	0.0335	239
0.010	800	0.022	364	0.034	235
0.0105	762	0.0225	356	0.0345	332
0.011	727	0.023	348	0.035	229
0.0115	696	0.0235	340	0.0355	225
0.012	667	0.024	333	0.036	222
0.0125	640	0.0245	327	0.0365	219
0.013	615	0.025	320	0.037	216
0.0135	593	0.0255	314	0.0375	213
0.014	571	0.026	308	0.038	211
0.0145	552	0.0265	302	0.0385	208
0.015	533	0.027	296	0.039	205
0.0155	516	0.0275	291	0.0395	203
0.016	500	0.028	286	0.040	200
0.0165	485	0.0285	281	0.0405	198
0.017	471	0.029	276	0.041	195
0.0175	457	0.0295	271	0.0415	193
0.018	444	0.030	267	0.042	190
0.0185	432	0.0305	262	0.0425	188

ness of four sheets of paper. In practice, a sheet folded twice to give four leafs or eight pages readies the paper for measurement. Four thicknesses of paper rather than one are measured in order to reduce the cumulative effect of multiplying small micrometer reading errors. The micrometer used for paper caliper measurements should have a vernier scale accurate enough to measure 0.0001 in.

Pages per Inch Equation

$$\text{Pages per inch} = \frac{8}{\text{Thickness of 4 sheets of paper}}$$

Example

If the thickness of four sheets of paper is 0.020 in., then:

$$\text{Pages per inch} = \frac{8}{0.020}$$

$$= 400$$

Book Thickness Equation

$$\text{Book thickness} = \frac{\text{No. of pages} \times \text{Thickness of 4 sheets}}{8}$$

Example

If the thickness of four sheets of paper is 0.028 in., then the thickness of an 860-page book is:

$$\text{Inches per page} = \frac{860 \times 0.028}{8.00}$$

$$= \frac{24.08}{8.00}$$

$$= 3.01 \text{ in.}$$

8 Cubic Area of Skids and Rolls

Paper consists in large measure of a fibrous material called cellulose. The papermaking process depends on cellulose fibers' strong attraction to water because only under the influence of water can cellulose fibers bond with each other to form sheets of paper during the papermaking process.

The transformation of cellulose fibers to paper never changes the fibers' inherent attraction to water, which leads to a host of potential problems during print production if certain conditions do not prevail or preventive measures are not taken.

To understand the dynamic forces of water vapor pressure in air and paper, it is necessary to clarify the concept of relative humidity (RH). RH is a measurement of the air's capacity to hold water vapor at different temperatures. The general principle is based on the fact that air can hold more water vapor at high temperatures than at low temperatures. When air is saturated with water vapor, sometimes called the dew point, 100% RH is reached. The mass of water vapor in saturated air at various temperatures is measurable and known. Therefore, the ratio of absolute water vapor in air, relative to the maximum amount that air can hold at a given temperature, can be calculated and constitutes the basis for relative humidity (Table 1.8.1).

Table 1.8.1.
Mass of water in saturated air.

Temperature		Grains/ Cubic Foot	Grams/ Cubic Meter
40°F	4.4°C	2.861	6.547
60	15.6	5.798	13.27
80	26.7	11.06	25.31
100	37.8	19.99	45.74

Central to the problem of relative humidity with regard to paper is the phenomenon of moisture exchange between paper and ambient air, when the relative humidity in paper and air is not the same. If the RH is lower in the paper than in the air, water vapor migrates from the air to the paper; conversely, if the RH is higher in the paper than in the air, water vapor migrates from the paper to the air. Both instances are detrimental to paper in that it changes its dimensions, especially in the cross-grain direction, because cellulose fibers change their size much more in their girth than in their length. Given the great precision required in close register printing, almost any amount of dimensional change detracts from printing quality and thus must be avoided. Moreover, these moisture exchanges cause paper to lose its flatness, which, in addition to unsightly products, also causes runnability problems on printing and finishing equipment.

Handling paper is fraught with dangers that can upset the desirable RH equilibrium between paper and air because RH changes in the paper are inevitable due to extreme temperature exposure during transport from the supplier to the printer. When paper is shipped to the printer, it will have a moisture content that results in approximate RH equilibrium in normal room temperature of about 75°F or 24°C, provided the temperature of the paper is also at room temperature. If, during transport, however, paper is exposed to extreme temperatures without further precautions, its RH also changes greatly, causing moisture loss or gain that is detrimental to the paper.

Wrapping the paper with materials that act as a moisture barrier preempts the described problems; even though extreme RH conditions may exist in the paper skid, moisture has nowhere to go and consequently no damage to the paper can occur.

Once paper has arrived at a pressroom, it may or may not have the same temperature as exists in the pressroom. Accurate temperature readings of paper can only be made with so-called sword thermometers, the probe of which is inserted into the pile.

The wrapping from reams, skids, and rolls of paper should only be removed when it has been determined that the temperature of the paper is identical to the environment in which it will be processed. Leaving the paper wrapped in the environment in which it will be used until it has the same temperature as this environment is called temperature conditioning and could take from a few hours to several days. Charts or tables can be used to determine the length of time required to temperature condition paper (Figures 1.8.1 and 1.8.2). This type of chart is interpreted on the basis of temperature differences between the paper and the paper processing environment, as well as the volume of a ream, skid, or roll of paper. The mathematical method for the latter variable, volume, is discussed in this section.

Figure 1.8.1.
Temperature conditioning chart for paper (nonmetric units).

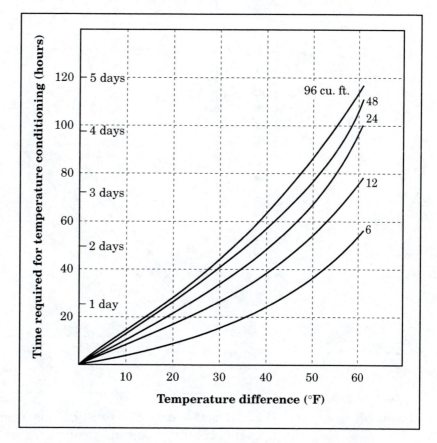

Adequate temperature and RH ranges for sheetfed printing are 70–85°F (21–29°C) and 35–50%, respectively. The midpoint of these ranges would be considered an optimal goal for temperature and RH.

Volume of a Skid Equation (Cubic Feet)

$$\text{Volume of a skid (in ft.}^3) = \frac{\text{Width} \times \text{Height} \times \text{Length}}{1{,}728}$$

where width, height, and length are in inches.

Figure 1.8.2.
Temperature
conditioning chart
for paper
(metric units).

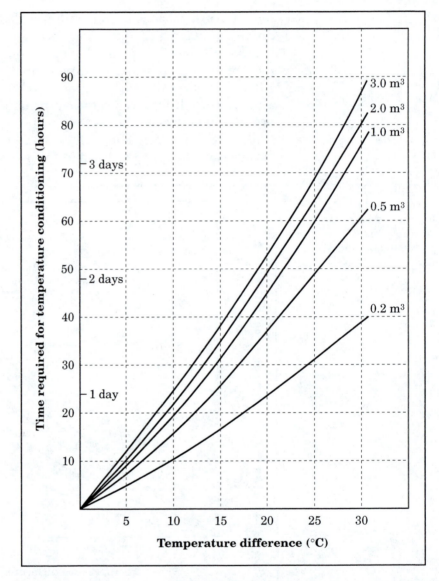

Example

If a skid measuring 20×28×74 in. has a temperature of 40°F, then determining the time required to temperature-condition this skid to an 80°F pressroom temperature is a three-step process, as shown below: (1) determine the volume of paper in the skid, (2) determine the difference in temperature between the paper and the pressroom, and (3) refer to Figure 1.8.1 to determine the hours of temperature conditioning required.

$$\text{Volume of the skid (ft.}^3) = \frac{20 \times 28 \times 74}{1{,}728}$$

$$= \frac{41,440}{1,728}$$

$$= 23.98$$

$$\approx 24 \text{ ft.}^3$$

$$\text{Pressroom temperature} = 80°\text{F}$$

$$\text{Paper temperature} = 40°\text{F}$$

$$\text{Temperature difference} = 80° - 40°$$

$$= 40°\text{F}$$

According to Figure 1.8.1, 24-ft.^{3} skids and 40°F temperature differences require approximately 50 hours of temperature conditioning time.

Volume of a Skid Equation (Cubic Meters)

$$\text{Volume of a skid (m}^3) = \frac{\text{Width} \times \text{Height} \times \text{Length}}{1,000,000}$$

where width, height, and length are in centimeters.

Example

If a skid measuring 98×174×60 cm has a temperature of 5°C, then determining the time required to temperature-condition this skid to a 35°C pressroom temperature is a three-step process, as shown below: (1) determine the volume of paper in the skid, (2) determine the difference in temperature between the paper and the pressroom, and (3) refer to Figure 1.8.2 to determine the hours of temperature conditioning required.

$$\text{Volume of the skid (m}^3) = \frac{98 \times 174 \times 60}{1,000,000}$$

$$= \frac{1,023,120}{1,000,000}$$

$$= 1.023$$

$$\approx 1.00 \text{ m}^3$$

$$\text{Pressroom temperature} = 35°C$$

$$\text{Paper temperature} = 5°C$$

$$\text{Temperature difference} = 35° - 5°$$

$$= 30°C$$

According to Figure 1.8.2, 1.00-m^3 skids and 30°C temperature differences require approximately 78 hours of temperature conditioning time.

Volume of a Roll Equation (Cubic Feet)

$$\text{Volume of a roll (ft.}^3) = \frac{(\text{Roll diameter})^2 \times \text{Roll width}}{2{,}200}$$

where roll diameter and roll width are in inches.

Example

If a roll with a diameter of 50 in. and a width of 42 in. has a temperature of 8°F, then determining the time required to temperature-condition this roll to a 28°F pressroom temperature is a three-step process: (1) determine the volume of paper in the roll, (2) determine the difference in temperature between the paper and the pressroom, and (3) refer to Figure 1.8.1 to determine the hours of temperature conditioning required.

$$\text{Volume of the roll (ft.}^3) = \frac{50^2 \times 42}{2{,}200}$$

$$= \frac{2{,}500 \times 42}{2{,}200}$$

$$= \frac{105{,}000}{2{,}200}$$

$$= 47.73$$

$$\approx 48 \text{ ft.}^3$$

$$\text{Pressroom temperature} = 28°F$$

$$\text{Paper temperature} = 8°F$$

$$\text{Temperature difference} = 28° - 8°$$

$$= 20°\text{F}$$

According to Figure 1.8.1, 48-ft.[3] rolls and 20°F temperature differences require approximately 26 hours of temperature conditioning time.

**Volume of a
Roll Equation
(Cubic Meters)**

$$\text{Volume of a roll (m}^3) = \frac{(\text{Roll diameter})^2 \times \text{Roll width}}{1{,}273{,}326}$$

where roll diameter and roll width are in centimeters.

Example

If a roll with a diameter of 70 cm and a width of 52 cm has a temperature of 10°C, then determining the time required to temperature-condition this roll to a 25°C pressroom temperature is a three-step process: (1) determine the volume of paper in the roll, (2) determine the difference in temperature between the paper and the pressroom, and (3) refer to Figure 1.8.2 to determine the hours of temperature conditioning required.

$$\text{Volume of the roll (m}^3) = \frac{70^2 \times 52}{1{,}273{,}326}$$

$$= \frac{4{,}900 \times 52}{1{,}273{,}326}$$

$$= \frac{254{,}800}{1{,}273{,}326}$$

$$= 0.200105864$$

$$\approx 0.200 \text{ m}^3$$

$$\text{Pressroom temperature} = 25°\text{C}$$

$$\text{Paper temperature} = 10°\text{C}$$

$$\text{Temperature difference} = 25° - 10°$$

$$= 15°\text{C}$$

According to Figure 1.8.2, 0.200-m^3 rolls and 15°C temperature differences require approximately 18 hours of temperature conditioning time.

9 Apparent Density

It is not unusual for papers with similar thicknesses or calipers to have dissimilar basis weights, or vice versa. This is explained by the varying degrees of denseness that different raw materials and papermaking processes impart on the paper. The denseness of paper has important ramifications for product suitability. For instance, an antique book paper requires low denseness, while a glassine paper has to be very dense in order to serve its purpose.

Grammage and basis weight do not take the caliper of paper into consideration; therefore, the caliper-to-weight ratio, and by logical extension the denseness of paper, is not determinable using these two weight measures. The apparent density of paper equation rises above these limitations because it allows calculation and comparison of paper weight that is based on a standard unit volume of one cubic centimeter.

Papers with low apparent density values have a high ratio of air to physical constituents, which is indicative of bulky and porous paper. High apparent density values are the attribute of less bulky and porous papers, resulting from high filler or short fiber content and papermaking process-related factors such as a combination of extensive fiber refinement, calendering, and wet pressing.

Apparent Density Equation

$$\text{Apparent density} = \frac{\text{Weight in grams per sq. meter} \times 0.001}{\text{Single sheet thickness (in mm)}}$$

Example 1

If a 90-g/m^2 sheet of paper has a thickness of 0.08 mm, the apparent density is:

$$\text{Apparent density} = \frac{90 \times 0.001}{0.08}$$

$$= \frac{0.09}{0.08}$$

$$= 1.125$$

Example 2   If a 90-g/m² sheet of paper has a thickness of 0.10 mm, the apparent density is:

$$\text{Apparent density} = \frac{90 \times 0.001}{0.10}$$

$$= \frac{0.09}{0.10}$$

$$= 0.900$$

Note that two papers with identical grammages can yield different apparent densities.

10 Roll Length from Known Diameter, Weight, and Width

Web printing's productivity and economy stems from extremely high printing speeds, sometimes exceeding 3,000 ft./min., and the pricing differential of roll paper as opposed to cartons or skids of sheet paper. Roll paper's lower price reflects reduced paper manufacturing cost, such as sheeting redundancy and simplified packaging requirements.

For this reason, some printers, particularly web printers with sheetfed capabilities, purchase rolls of paper for sheetfed presses. This practice, while reducing the cost of paper, requires either offline sheeting equipment or roll-to-sheet feeders integrated with a sheetfed press. Paper purchased in rolls for sheetfed production affords the additional advantage of size flexibility because the cutoff length in the machine direction can be virtually any size, thus eliminating selective purchase and storage of different paper sizes.

Unlike paper purchased in sheets, the number of cutoff lengths in a roll are usually not immediately apparent and must therefore be estimated using the mathematical method discussed in this section. Some papermakers make estimates of roll length or square footage data available to the printer, but it is far more common for the papermaker to supply only roll weight, basis weight, roll width, and paper classification information.

The extreme long runs that are the norm in web printing make it absolutely necessary to determine the linear length of a roll; otherwise, it would not be possible to purchase the quantity of rolls required for a given number of impressions or cutoff lengths.

Purchasing more rolls than are necessary ties up financial resources. Purchasing quantities of rolls that come up short to complete a job can lead to a failure of complying with vital deadlines, which is particularly serious with periodical publications.

In web printing a cutoff length is synonymous with a single impression and cannot normally be changed because cutoff lengths are fixed.

Linear Feet and Impressions per Roll from Known Roll Diameter, Weight, and Width Equations

$$\text{Linear feet of a roll} = \frac{\text{Roll weight} \times \text{Area of basic size} \times 500}{\text{Roll width} \times 12 \times \text{Basis weight}}$$

where the area of basic size is given in Table 1.1.1, and roll width is in inches.

$$\text{Impressions per roll} = \frac{\text{Linear feet of roll} \times 12}{\text{Cutoff length (in inches)}}$$

Example

If a 35-in.-wide roll of 50-lb. offset paper weighs 1,225 lb., then the linear feet and number of impressions that can be obtained from this roll if printed on a web press with a 22.25-in. cutoff are:

$$\text{Linear feet of this roll} = \frac{1,225 \times 950 \times 500}{35 \times 12 \times 50}$$

$$= \frac{581,875,000}{21,000}$$

$$= 27,708.33333$$

$$\text{Impressions from this roll} = \frac{27,708.33333 \times 12}{22.25}$$

$$= \frac{332,500}{22.25}$$

$$= 14,943.82022$$

$$\approx 14,943$$

11 Roll Length from Known Diameter and Paper Caliper

The stated objective of this method is identical to the linear feet and impressions per roll equations discussed in section 10, but the known variables from which the roll length is calculated are the roll diameter, core diameter, and paper caliper. Papermakers usually supply roll diameter data, in the absence of which it could simply be measured with a tape measure. Roll cores could be of the returnable or non-returnable variety. They must match the chuck size employed on a particular press and as such are a known quantity. If paper caliper information is not provided it can be measured with a micrometer affording fourth decimal place accuracy.

Linear Length and Impressions per Roll from Known Roll Diameter and Paper Caliper Equations

Linear feet of a roll =
$$\frac{65.45 \times [(\text{Roll diameter})^2 - (\text{Core diameter})^2]}{\text{Paper caliper} \times 1{,}000}$$

where roll diameter, core diameter, and paper caliper are in inches.

Linear meters of a roll =
$$\frac{78.54 \times [(\text{Roll diameter})^2 - (\text{Core diameter})^2]}{\text{Paper caliper}}$$

where roll diameter and core diameter are in centimeters, and paper caliper is in millimeters.

$$\text{Impressions per roll (inches)} = \frac{\text{Linear feet of roll} \times 12}{\text{Cutoff length (in inches)}}$$

$$\text{Impressions per roll (meters)} = \frac{\text{Linear meters of roll} \times 100}{\text{Cutoff length (in centimeters)}}$$

Example 1   If a roll has a diameter of 40 in., a core diameter of 4 in., and a paper caliper of 0.004 in., then the linear feet and impressions that can be obtained from this roll, if printed on a web press with 22.25-in. cutoff, are:

$$\text{Linear feet of this roll} = \frac{65.45 \, (40^2 - 4^2)}{0.004 \times 1,000}$$

$$= \frac{65.45 \, (1,600 - 16)}{0.004 \times 1,000}$$

$$= \frac{65.45 \times 1,584}{0.004 \times 1,000}$$

$$= \frac{103,672.8}{0.004 \times 1,000}$$

$$= \frac{103,672.8}{4}$$

$$= 25,918.2$$

$$\text{Impressions from this roll} = \frac{25,918.2 \times 12}{22.25}$$

$$= \frac{311,018.4}{22.25}$$

$$= 13,978.35506$$

$$\approx 13,978$$

Example 2   If the roll, paper, and cutoff measurements in example 1 are converted to metric values, then roll diameter is 101.6 cm, core diameter is 10.16 cm, paper caliper is 0.1016 mm, and the cutoff is 56.515 cm. Linear meters and impressions per roll are calculated as follows:

$$\text{Linear meters per roll} = \frac{78.54 \, (101.6^2 - 10.16^2)}{0.1016 \times 1,000}$$

$$= \frac{78.54\,(10{,}322.56 - 103.2256)}{0.1016 \times 1{,}000}$$

$$= \frac{78.54 \times 10{,}219.3344}{0.1016 \times 1{,}000}$$

$$= \frac{802{,}626.5238}{0.1016 \times 1{,}000}$$

$$= \frac{802{,}626.5238}{101.6}$$

$$= 7{,}899.86736$$

$$\text{Impressions from this roll} = \frac{7{,}899.86736 \times 100}{56.515}$$

$$= \frac{789{,}986.736}{56.515}$$

$$= 13{,}978.35506$$

$$\approx 13{,}978$$

Please note that the imperial and metric values yield an identical number of impressions.

12 Roll Weight in Pounds

The great printing speed of web printing renders it imma-
nently suitable for high-volume printing, hence run lengths
of several million impressions are not unusual in this very
productive printing industry sector.

Paper costs as a proportion of total printing production
costs increase significantly with these long run lengths and
must therefore be judiciously controlled and calculated.

Since the printer paid for the paper rolls according to their
weight, the weight of rolls consumed during a print run also
becomes a criterion for pricing a job.

Papermakers, as a rule, will make roll weights available to
the printer, in paper catalogs and on labels affixed to roll
wrappings. However, when a job is printed with rest (stub)
rolls from previous runs, this weight information is no longer
relevant and the only other methods at the printer's disposal
are to either weigh the roll on a scale or to use the mathematical method discussed in this section. In practice,
weighing the rolls is cumbersome because of the handling
required, thus the mathematical method of determining roll
weight provides a quick and convenient alternative.

To calculate the weight of a roll it is necessary to determine the roll and core diameters with a tape measure and to
use constant factors that correspond with one of nine types of
paper listed in Table 1.12.1.

The constant factors were empirically determined in consideration of paper having different weight-to-roll diameter
ratios, depending on their classification or finish. Referring
to Table 1.12.1, it can be seen that porous and bulky antique
finished papers have lower constant factor values than more
dense and compact coated two-sided papers. Once again this
serves to remind us that paper thickness or diameter, as is
the case with rolls, is no indication of weight, unless the

Table 1.12.1.
Roll factors for roll
weight calculations.

Antique finish	0.018
Vellum office	0.020
Bond	0.021
Regular offset	0.022
Machine finish	0.026
English finish book	0.027
Supercalendered	0.028
Coated 1-side	0.030
Coated 2-sides	0.033

weight per unit cubic area is taken into account. (For further information on apparent density, refer to section 9.) The constant factors effectively compensate for any difference of paper denseness that invariably exists with different types of papers.

**Roll Weight
Equation**

Roll weight =
$$[(\text{Roll diameter})^2 - (\text{Core diameter})^2] \times \text{Roll width} \times \text{RF}$$

where RF is the *roll factor* (according to Table 1.12.1.).

$$\text{Price per CWT} = \frac{\text{Total weight in pounds} \times \text{CWT price}}{100}$$

For further information on paper cost calculations using CWT, refer to section 6.

Example

If a 35-in.-wide roll of regular offset paper has a diameter of 40 in., a core diameter of 3.5 in., and the CWT price for this roll paper is $89.56, then the cost of this roll is:

$$\text{Roll weight} = (40 - 3.5) \times 35 \times 0.022$$

$$= (1{,}600 - 12.25) \times 35 \times 0.022$$

$$= 1{,}587.75 \times 35 \times 0.022$$

$$= 1{,}222.5675$$

$$\approx 1{,}223 \text{ lb.}$$

$$\text{Price per CWT} = \frac{1{,}223 \times 89.56}{100}$$

$$= \frac{109{,}531.88}{100}$$

$$= \$1{,}095.32$$

13   Sheet Optimization

The practice of printing the same image content multiple times on a press sheet is sometimes called printing four, six, sixteen, etc. "times up," depending on the number of times the image content is repeated on a press sheet.

Printing multiple "times up" is particularly useful when printing small image areas such as the quintessential postage stamp, because every image content repeat brings an equal and opposite reduction in run length. Furthermore, very small images must necessarily be printed multiple times up because their size might be smaller than the minimum size that can be accommodated on a sheetfed press. An additional advantage of printing multiple times up is that the benefits derived in the press area carry over to subsequent finishing processes. For example, a job such as invoice pads printed two-up would cut in half the amount of time needed to pad, collate, perforate, or number the pads.

Given these circumstances, a paper size that results in the least amount of waste when printing multiple times up is the option for which a printer should strive. Extraneous amounts of paper that are not converted into printed products were paid for by the printer but should not be charged to the customer if the waste is avoidable and unnecessary.

The large number of standard sizes offered by paper merchants provides an opportunity to minimize waste by selecting a size that optimizes the printable area.

Beyond optimization of paper areas, other aspects such as size limitations of the printing press and the grain direction requirements of the finished printed piece have to be ascertained.

Grain direction in particular must suit the process and end-use requirements of printed pieces. The terms commonly used to describe paper grain directions are *grain long* and *grain short* for grain directions that run parallel to the long or short edges of the paper, respectively.

The preferred grain direction for book pages with a portrait or upright orientation is grain long, while book pages with landscape or oblong orientation require grain-short pages. This reduces the risk for rippling and improves adhesion in the perfect binding process. Moreover, pages with the grain direction parallel to the book's backbone lay flatter when opened, thus improving readability. This is but one of many instances in which grain direction has a bearing on product quality; a decision as to the correct grain direction for various products must be made on a case-by-case basis.

Papermakers communicate grain direction in one of three ways. The grain direction could be indicated in the narrative, stating a paper as being "grain long" or grain short. In paper catalogs an explanatory sentence often states that the second dimension indicates the grain direction, which is to say a 17×22-in. paper is grain long and a 22×17-in. paper is grain short. Finally, an underscored dimension could indicate grain direction, which means a 17×22 notation is grain long and a 17×22 notation is grain short.

Optimizing sheet areas always starts with determining the grain direction requirements of a finished job. If the small sheets' grain direction must be identical to the grain direction of the large sheets from which they are cut, then the long and short dimensions of the small sheet must be divided into the long and short dimensions of the large sheet, respectively. The results of both divisions are then multiplied with each other, disregarding the fractional remainders, to give the maximum number of sheets that can be cut from the large sheet (Figure 1.13.1). Conversely, if the small sheets' grain direction must be opposite to the grain direction of the large sheets from which they are cut, then the long and short directions of the small sheet must be divided into the short and long directions of the large sheet, respectively. Here again the results are multiplied with each other, disregarding the fractional remainders (Figure 1.13.2).

If the grain direction is of no consequence for a particular product, then the result that yields the largest number of "sheets out" is the optimal solution.

There is yet another method of optimizing paper areas that is not easily defined in mathematical terms because it entails true optimization of mixed grain directions on the same large sheet. This solution is only viable when grain direction is of no concern or if the result yields sufficient numbers in both grain directions for two or more jobs that have different grain direction requirements. To find the number of mixed-grain sheets that can be cut from a large sheet, it is in practice necessary to use a trial-and-error method of drawing cutting diagrams that often results in more "sheets out" than the two methods described previously (Figure 1.13.3). This method, if viable, optimizes the printable area of a press sheet to an absolute maximum and could result in considerable paper cost reductions.

Computer programs with algorithms entailing hundreds of iterations can be used to accomplish this task, sparing printers the tedious task of drawing multiple diagrams. The software included with this book includes such a function.

Sheet Optimization Equations

Small and large sheet will have identical grain directions.

$$X = \frac{\text{Large sheet short dimension}}{\text{Small sheet short dimension}}$$

$$Y = \frac{\text{Large sheet long dimension}}{\text{Small sheet long dimension}}$$

No. of sheets $= X \times Y$

where X and Y are rounded down to the nearest integer.

Small and large sheet will have opposite grain directions.

$$X = \frac{\text{Large sheet short dimension}}{\text{Small sheet long dimension}}$$

$$Y = \frac{\text{Large sheet long dimension}}{\text{Small sheet short dimension}}$$

No. of sheets $= X \times Y$

where X and Y are rounded down to the nearest integer.

Waste % =

$$100 - \frac{\text{Square area of small sheet} \times \text{No. of sheets out} \times 100}{\text{Square area of large sheet}}$$

Example 1   If a 28½×45-in. printing bristol is cut down to 4×6-in. post-cards, then the maximum number of postcards that can be obtained, if the postcards have to be grain short, is:

$$X = \frac{28.5}{4}$$

$$= 7.125$$

$$\approx 7$$

$$Y = \frac{45}{6}$$

$$= 7.5000$$

$$\approx 7$$

$$\text{Postcards out} = 7 \times 7$$

$$= 49$$

$$\text{Waste \%} = 100 - \frac{4 \times 6 \times 49 \times 100}{28.5 \times 45}$$

Figure 1.13.1.
The maximum number of postcards that can be obtained if the postcards have to be grain short.

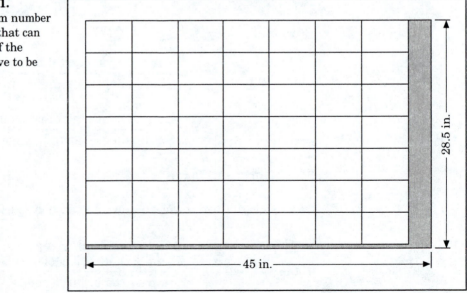

$$= 100 - \frac{117,600}{1,282.5}$$

$$= 100 - 91.69590643$$

$$= 8.304035700$$

$$\approx 8.3\%$$

Example 2   If a 28½×45-in. printing bristol is cut down to 4×6-in. post-cards, then the maximum number of postcards that can be obtained, if the postcards have to be grain long, is:

$$X = \frac{28.5}{6}$$

$$= 4.7500$$

$$\approx 4$$

$$Y = \frac{45}{4}$$

$$= 11.2500$$

$$\approx 11$$

Figure 1.13.2.
The maximum number of postcards that can be obtained if the postcards have to be grain long.

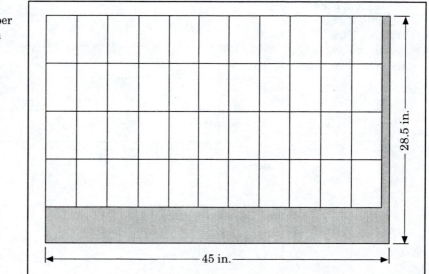

28.5 in.

45 in.

$$\text{Postcards out} = 4 \times 11$$

$$= 44$$

$$\text{Waste \%} = 100 - \frac{4 \times 6 \times 44 \times 100}{28.5 \times 45}$$

$$= 100 - \frac{105,600}{1,282.5}$$

$$= 100 - 82.33918129$$

$$= 17.66081871$$

$$\approx 17.66\%$$

Example 3

If a 28½×45-in. printing bristol is cut down to 4×6-in. post-cards, then the maximum number of postcards that can be obtained, if the postcards could have mixed grain directions, is determined by using a trial-and-error method or a sheet optimization computer program. In this example, the maximum number of postcards out of the 28½×45-in. sheet is 51.

$$\text{Waste \%} = 100 - \frac{6 \times 4 \times 51 \times 100}{28.5 \times 45}$$

Figure 1.13.3.
The maximum number of postcards that can be obtained if the postcards could have mixed grain directions.

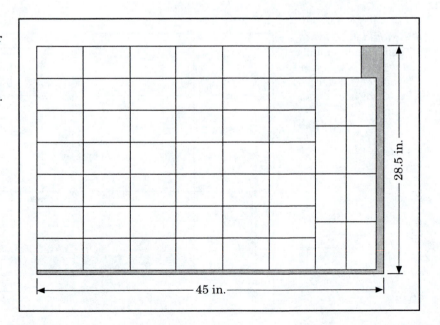

$$= 100 - \frac{122,400}{1,282.5}$$

$$= 100 - 95.43859649$$

$$= 4.561403510$$

$$\approx 4.56\%$$

14 ABC System of International Paper Sizes

If we look around us, almost all printed pieces—be they books, posters, stationery, labels, or postcards—have rectangular shapes. Art historians have traced this tendency to represent graphic images within rectangular boundaries to the height to width proportions of the human figure. As far back as classical antiquity, artists and mathematicians were intrigued by the perfect relations of a rectangle, which in the Renaissance came to be known as the "Golden Section" or the "Divine Proportions."

The Golden Section can be described by the following equation: AC/AB = CB/AC, where A and B are the terminal points of a line and C is a point on this line. This ratio has the numeric value of 0.618 (Figure 1.14.1).

Figure 1.14.1.
The Golden Section ratio of length to height.

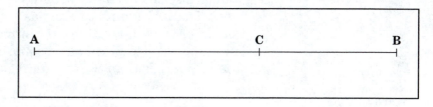

The Golden Section is truly a form of standardization or, more precisely, a method to standardize an aesthetic ideal.

The international paper sizes conform only partly to this aesthetic ideal in that they are still rectangular in shape, albeit at not quite the same proportions as the Golden Section.

The impetus for the international paper sizes grew mostly out of a desire to develop a system of practical standard paper sizes for industrial applications to replace the vast variety of paper formats that existed at the time. Standard paper sizes were established in Germany in the 1920s by the

Deutsche Institut für Normung, or the German Standard Institute, and were subsequently adopted by the International Standards Organization (ISO) in Switzerland as the ISO 216 paper size system. It proposes the following guidelines:

- Paper sizes are expressed in metric values.
- All paper sizes have a height to width ratio of $1{:}\sqrt{2}$ or 1:1.4142.
- The basic format A0 has a square area of 1 m^2.
- The next smaller size from a given standard size is exactly half its square area. The long edge of the smaller size will have the same length as the short edge of the next larger size, while the short edge of the smaller size will be exactly half the size as the long edge of the next larger size (Figure 1.14.2).
- The standard height and width for the trimmed A and B series is a rounded number of millimeters (Table 1.14.1), and in the untrimmed RA and SRA series a rounded number of millimeters (Table 1.14.3).
- The standard series A and B are trimmed dimensions of the final end product. The A series is the most widely used, while the B series was introduced as intermediate sizes to afford printers more choice.
- The standard series C is for envelopes (Table 1.14.1).
- Standard series RA and SRA are for untrimmed paper. The RA0 standard size has a square area of 1.05 m^2 or is 5% larger than the standard size A0. The standard size SRA0 has a square area of 1.15 m^2 or is 15% larger than the standard size A0.

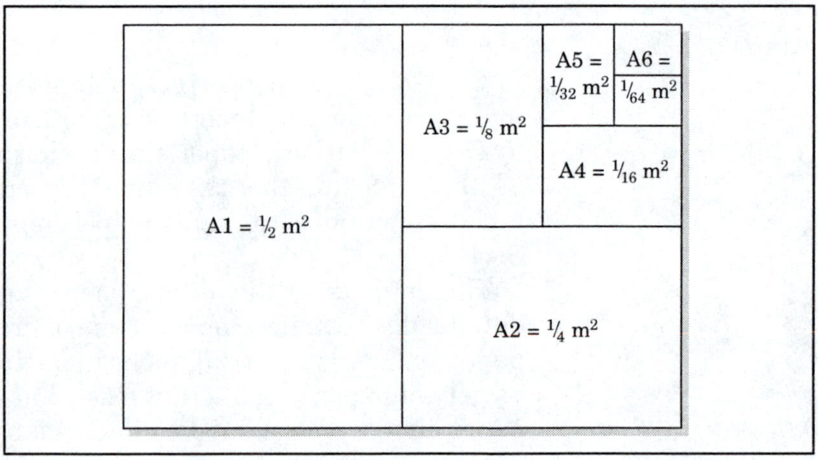

Figure 1.14.2.
An ISO A0 sheet having a square area of 1 m^2, subdivided into successively smaller A series sizes, showing their respective fractional part of a square meter.

A1 = $\frac{1}{2}$ m²

A3 = $\frac{1}{8}$ m²

A5 = $\frac{1}{32}$ m²   A6 = $\frac{1}{64}$ m²

A4 = $\frac{1}{16}$ m²

A2 = $\frac{1}{4}$ m²

Table 1.14.1.
ISO A and B trimmed paper sizes and C envelope sizes.

A Series Paper Sizes		B Series Paper Sizes		C Series Envelope Sizes	
4A0	1,682×2,378	—	—	—	—
2A0	1,189×1,682	—	—	—	—
A0	841×1,189	B0	1,000×1,414	C0	916×1,297
A1	594×841	B1	707×1,000	C1	648×917
A2	420×594	B2	500×707	C2	458×648
A3	297×420	B3	353×500	C3	324×458
A4	210×297	B4	250×353	C4	229×324
A5	148×210	B5	176×250	C5	162×229
A6	105×148	B6	125×176	C6	114×162
A7	74×105	B7	88×125	C7	81×114
A8	52×74	B8	62×88	C8	57×81
A9	37×52	B9	44×62	C9	40×57
A10	26×37	B10	31×44	C10	28×40

It will be noted that calculated square areas are not exactly the same as the nominally stated values. The reason is related to the rounding that takes place, which results in a calculated A0 square area of 0.999949 m^2 (841×1,189), instead of the nominally stated 1 m^2, for example. In practice these small differences are not large enough to cause significant problems.

The use of standard sizes for particular paper products has tremendous advantages, not only for the printer who will be able to cut paper products from larger standard sizes with a minimum of waste, but also for manufacturers of auxiliary products such as leather portfolios for personal stationery, wallets with business card and credit card pockets,

Table 1.14.2.
Typical products and their corresponding ISO paper series designation.

ISO Paper Series	Typical Applications
A0, A1	Posters, technical drawings, maps
A2, A3	Diagrams, drawings, large tablets
A4	Stationery, magazines, catalogs, forms, laser and inkjet printer copying paper
A5	Notepads
A6	Postcards
B5, A5, B6, A6	Books
B4, A3	Tabloid newspapers
C4, C5, C6	Envelopes for A4 stationery, unfolded (C4), folded once (C5), folded twice (C6)

briefcases with pockets for several common paper products, etc., by not having to manufacture these products in a multitude of different sizes.

European usage of standard paper sizes extends to a wide and growing variety of products ranging from the European Union passport (B7), to the German citizen I.D. (A7), to library microfiches (A6), and even toilet paper (A6).

Table 1.14.3.
ISO RA and SRA untrimmed paper sizes. (All sizes are in millimeters.)

RA Series Sizes		SRA Series Sizes	
RA0	860×1,220	SRA0	900×1,280
RA1	610×860	SRA1	640×900
RA2	430×610	SRA2	450×640
RA3	305×430	SRA3	320×450
RA4	215×305	SRA4	225×320

Some of these standard sizes are again shown in Table 1.14.2 to list some typical products and their respective standard sizes.

In order to cut large sheets into smaller sizes accurately and cleanly, the large sheet must have a trim area around its four edges. This is to say, if A0 sheets have to be cut down to A4 sheets, a sheet having dimensions that are somewhat larger than the A0 sheet is required. This is the purpose of the RA and SRA series, which are both larger than their respective A series counterparts (Table 1.14.3).

A series paper sizes, by virtue of their A0 square area of 1 m^2 paper, are conducive to the grammage method of paper

Figure 1.14.3.
An ISO A0 sheet weighing 96 grams, subdivided into successively smaller A series sizes, showing their respective weights in grams.

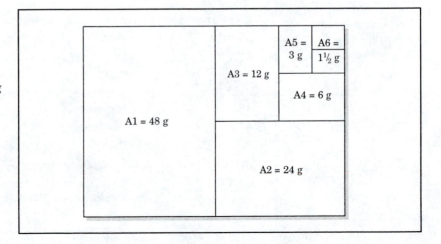

weight calculations, which is also based on a sheet's weight of per 1 m^2 (for further information on grammage, refer to section 1). To further illustrate this point, Figure 1.14.3 shows an A0 sheet with the A series sizes up to A6 and their respective weights in grams.

In general, the international sizes have been adopted throughout the world with the notable exception of Canada and the United States, where, for example, the letter size 8.5×11 in. and other nonmetric paper sizes dominate. Adoption of the international paper sizes is slowly being made in places like universities, because of their exposure to international magazines and conferences which often require papers and proceedings to be submitted in A4 format.

Missing Dimension Equations

$$\text{Missing width dimension} = \frac{\text{Height dimension}}{\sqrt{2}}$$

$$\text{Missing height dimension} = \text{Width dimension} \times \sqrt{2}$$

Example 1

If the height dimension of a B series size is 707 mm, then its width dimension is:

$$\text{Missing width dimension} = \frac{707}{\sqrt{2}}$$

$$= \frac{707}{1.414213562}$$

$$= 499.9244944$$

$$\approx 500 \text{ mm}$$

Example 2

If the width dimension of an A series size is 841, the height dimension is:

$$\text{Missing height dimension} = 841 \times \sqrt{2}$$

$$= 841 \times 1.414213562$$

$$= 1189.353606$$

$$\approx 1189 \text{ mm}$$

Note: the Results can be verified in Table 1.14.1.

Total Weight Equation

Total weight = Weight of desired A series sheet ×
Trim × No. of sheets required

where *Trim* = 1   for cutting from A series sheets
= 1.05 for cutting from RA series sheets
= 1.15 for cutting from SRA series sheets

Example

If 18,000 A6 postcards are cut from RA0 bristol board sheets having a grammage of 120 g/m^2, the total weight of the postcards is:

Since an A6 sheet weighs ¹⁄₆₄ of an A0 sheet, one A6 sheet weighs

$$= \frac{120}{64}$$

$$= 1.875$$

Total weight $= 1.875 \times 1.05 \times 18{,}000$

$$= 35437.5 \text{ g}$$

$$= 35.4375 \text{ kg}$$

$$\approx 35.4 \text{ kg}$$

Part 2
Print

Modern conventional printing equipment productivity is unsurpassed, especially in the medium to long production run ranges. Production speeds of 15,000 impressions per hour for sheetfed and 50,000 impressions per hour for webfed equipment are now possible, even as job complexities are increased to more than the standard four colors, perfecting, and in-line finishing. Greater automation has also resulted in drastically reduced manpower requirements. Only twenty years ago four-color presses were manned by four operators, while today two operators are the norm.

This combination of greatly increased production speeds, higher job complexity, and a reduced number of operators manning the equipment necessitates fast initial attainment and consistent maintenance of automatically measured numeric print quality aimpoints. Current market trends are toward shorter run lengths. Because the proportional significance of the makeready phase increases as run length decreases, greater automation that reduces makeready times becomes imperative.

The principal instruments for print quality measurements are densitometers, spectrophotometers, and register control devices. At the highest level of automation, these instruments can scan the output of a press automatically and compare measured print characteristic values with digitally stored reference values. If a measured value is beyond predetermined tolerances the system will respond automatically by sending signals to the appropriate press controls. These press controls in turn respond automatically with actions such as moving printing cylinders to correct image misregister or adjusting zonal ink keys to correct image quality characteristics such as density, gray balance, or several other measurable and standardized values.

These quality systems depend entirely on numeric data, because they are essentially microprocessor-controlled. Press operators and quality control personnel require an intimate knowledge of numeric print characteristic standards, as these highly automated systems still require the human input of setting the reference values for particular production parameters such as quality levels, paper, and ink.

Given that the typical print characteristic values for a particular press system are communicated to the prepress area, where they can be compensated, a highly automated and standardized press production environment should be capable of producing any job satisfactorily with a single set of print characteristic values.

This part of the book contains ten sections that discuss the major measurable print characteristics, while four sections deal with printing or pressroom calculations that are unrelated to instrumental quality control.

1 Total Dot Gain

The reproduction of images with tonal ranges such as photographs requires a continuous-tone image to be converted into halftones. This is true for virtually all printing processes and effectively breaks the original continuous-tone image into dots of varying sizes, such as in conventional halftones, or into dots of equal size that are more or less clustered, as in the more recently developed stochastic screening processes. In either case, the tonal range of an original is reproduced by means of dots that are sufficiently small so as not to be discernible as individual dots but instead are perceived as shades of gray or shades of a color. In fact, it can be said that almost all printing processes are capable of reproducing only one shade of black or color. The apparent shades are really an optical illusion created by a series of very small and closely spaced dots.

It is thus of crucial importance to the fidelity of a reproduction that dot sizes are controlled, because even miniscule halftone dot size changes have great effects on the tonal values of the reproduction.

For better understanding it is useful at this time to introduce a fundamental definition of dot gain and then proceed to the various process stages where the dot sizes are subject to changes. Dot gain simply means the difference of the measured dot area on a printed press sheet to the measured dot area on the film. Therefore, the reference value for dot gain is always the original film dot value.

The instruments used to measure dot values on film and printing substrates are the transmission and reflection densitometers, respectively. Densitometers fundamentally yield densities, and since the total dot gain equation is a function of density, total dot gain can be derived mathematically in the internal circuitry of the densitometer or by manual calculation.

Since it would be extremely cumbersome to measure actual halftone film dot areas, and virtually impossible to measure precisely the same areas on a press sheet, we make all measurements on a print control strip that is placed on the same flat as the halftone in such a way that it falls in a trim area. Print control strips, also known as color control bars, are available in positive or negative form and are manufactured to produce nominal dot areas to very close tolerances. Common dot areas found on print control strips are 25, 50, and 75%. The validity of making dot size measurements on control strip patches of known dot sizes is based on the certainty that the dot sizes on the control strip invariably also exist in the halftone film to be reproduced. We can thus be sure that any dot size change measured on the print control strip also applies to the equivalent dot area in the printed image itself.

A word of caution: this statement is only true if original control strips are used; any attempts to duplicate control strips will invariably result in faulty measurements, since it is virtually impossible to maintain the original dot sizes in the duplicating process. Also, the line screen ruling of the control strip must be of the same fineness as the halftone to be reproduced, because line screen ruling is yet another factor that affects the amount of dot gain. Higher line screen rulings produce significantly greater dot gain than lower line screen rulings.

The vast majority of reproductions are produced today in the offset lithographic process on plates that were imaged from negatives; therefore, typical values produced under these conditions will serve as examples. Similar results, if not in detail but in principle, can be expected under different conditions or when different printing processes are involved.

In the course of the different printing production phases, the first instance of dot size change occurs when the plate is exposed through the negative and subsequently developed by chemical processes. A 50% film dot area will normally grow by 2% to become a 52% dot area on the plate.

The offset lithographic printing process, not unlike other conventional printing processes, requires pressure to transfer an inked image to the substrate. This, combined with the fact that the ink is a pasty liquid, results in the inked dots being squeezed beyond their original image area confines.

This usually causes an additional dot enlargement of 10%. Added to the previous 2% dot enlargement, the 50% film dot area will now have a physical size of 62% on the substrate, which is why we speak of the physical dot area at this stage.

The final dot enlargement is an optical phenomenon that is due to light penetrating between the dots that is trapped under the dots and thus absorbed. It causes the dot to appear about 12% optically larger than its physical size (Figure 2.1.1). The densitometer is as sensitive to this optical enlargement as is the human eye, and consequently this optical phenomenon is measurable. Adding this last optical enlargement to the previous two physical enlargements, we now have a dot area of 74%. This is called total dot area.

Figure 2.1.1.
Optical dot gain.

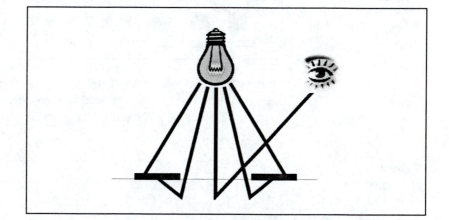

To calculate total dot gain we simply subtract the original film dot value from the total dot area value (74% – 50% = 24%), and we arrive at a total dot gain value of 24%.

A 24% dot gain may appear to be an excessive increase, but it is considered normal for sheetfed offset printing from negative plates on coated paper, according to published standards.

This amount of dot gain should not, however, be construed as an acceptable tonal increase for a midtone area of the original. Instead, it must be seen as an unavoidable dot value increase that is inherent in printing processes, which is anticipated and compensated in the digital prepress stages. This is to say that the 50% film dot area is the result of digital prepress compensation in order to produce a 74% shadow area on the reproduction.

Most standards for printing production specify allowable tolerances for midtone values only, because it is here where the greatest dot gain is experienced. The reason is one of simple geometry. Dot gain can really only occur at the edges or border zones of dots, and these edges have the longest peripheral length at the 50% checkerboard midtone dot. It follows that dot gain must be greatest in 50% dots and less in the 25% and 75% dot areas because the peripheral lengths of their border zones are similarly shortened (Figure 2.1.2).

Figure 2.1.2.
Border zone theory. The dotted border zones signify dot sizes after dot gain has occurred. Note that the total area gained is greater in the 50% dot area than in the 25% and 75% dot areas.

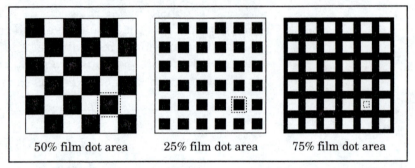

50% film dot area	25% film dot area	75% film dot area

It is for this reason that dot gain, when plotted on a graph, will produce the characteristic symmetrical curve with the apex of the curve indicating dot gain in the 50% film dot area (Figure 2.1.3).

Figure 2.1.3.
Dot gain curve. Four-color dot gain curve with 4% range at the 50% dot.

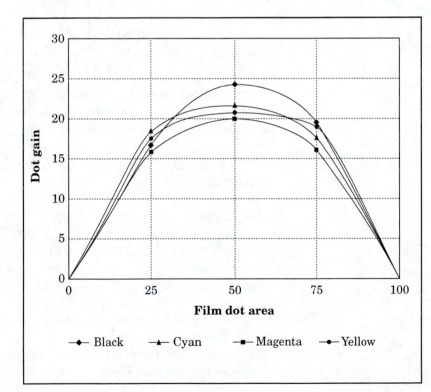

Another area of concern is the effect that dot gain has on color balance in four-color process printing. Simply stated, dot gain in all four colors and especially the three chromatic colors should be identical. If any of the process colors produces a significantly different dot gain value, severe color shifts are sure to follow. Since a zero dot gain range is practically not achievable, most published standards allow a 4% dot gain range between the colors. For example, dot gain values of cyan 20%, magenta 22%, yellow 18%, and black 22% would be at the upper limit of acceptability.

While a 4% dot gain spread between the colors has been shown to be acceptable for most originals with a normal chromatic range, some research, notably by Felix Brunner, has shown that certain extremely chromatic originals such as a bouquet of flowers can tolerate as much as a 6% dot gain range. Other very achromatic originals such as a snowy scene can tolerate only a 2% dot gain range between colors before noticeable color shifts occur.

The general rule for dot gain control is to consistently aim for and maintain standard dot gain values with as little dot gain range between the colors as possible.

Murray/Davies Total Dot Area Equation

$$\text{Total dot area} = 100 \times \left(\frac{1 - 10^{-\text{Tint}}}{1 - 10^{-\text{Solid}}} \right)$$

where *tint* is the net density of a tint and *solid* is the net density of a solid.

For total dot area measurements on press sheets, the tint and solid ink densities should preferably be taken in the same ink zone or in close proximity to each other. Net density means density minus paper density.

$$\text{Total dot gain} = \text{Total dot area} - \text{Film dot area}$$

where *film dot area* is the film dot area that produced the equivalent total dot area on the substrate.

Example

Suppose a 75% print control strip patch and a neighboring solid ink density patch yield densities of 0.95 and 1.39, respectively, then:

$$\text{Total dot area} = 100 \times \left(\frac{1 - 10^{-0.95}}{1 - 10^{-1.39}} \right)$$

$$= 100 \times \left(\frac{1 - 0.112201845}{1 - 0.040738027}\right)$$

$$= 100 \times \left(\frac{0.887798155}{0.959261973}\right)$$

$$= 100 \times 0.9255$$

$$= 92.55$$

$$\approx 93\%$$

The 75% print control patch was measured, therefore:

$$\text{Total dot gain} = 93 - 75$$

$$= 18\%$$

2   Physical Dot Gain

Total dot gain (described in the preceding section) is so called because it includes both physical and optical dot gain. Logically, the definition of physical dot gain is optical dot gain subtracted from total dot gain. As has been described in the preceding section, optical dot gain is a function of the substrate's propensity to trap light that penetrates between the halftone dots. This optical phenomenon causes dot sizes that are larger than could have been caused by their physical size alone (Figure 2.1.1).

The physical dot area equation is identical to the total dot area equation in all aspects, save for the inclusion of a constant factor called the n-factor. The n-factor's function is to effectively subtract the optical dot gain component from the total dot area.

Generally, newsprint and uncoated papers are more prone to optical dot gain than coated papers, and most non-fibrous substrates such as offset lithographic printing plates have an even lower tendency for optical dot gain than both coated and uncoated papers.

Hence, the value of an n-factor depends on the light-trapping property of a substrate, which has been determined empirically for a number of broad substrate classifications.

Physical dot gain measurements are relevant in print-quality analysis, especially when the cause of dot gain on printing plates is investigated. Because the optical dot area component of halftone dots on a printing plate has no capacity to transfer to the substrate, the physical dot area equation must be used when making halftone dot measurements on printing plates. Other areas of relevancy are print-quality analyses of paper and proofs in order to identify factors that contribute to dot growth, other than the optical effect of substrates.

A more accurate measurement method of physical dot areas than previously described involves the use of a planimeter, but because of its considerable cost, it is used only in scientific research. It has been found that the densitometer combined with a physical dot gain function built into its internal circuitry or manual calculations converting densities to physical dot area is reasonably accurate for most printing production purposes.

Here again a word of caution when making physical dot area measurements on plates: Densitometers yield only accurate results when process colors are measured, while the uninked color of plate image areas is often a non-process color. Consequently, accurate results cannot be expected under these circumstances. An approximate accuracy is possible, however, when the densitometer filter channel that produces the highest reading is used.

Yule/Nielson Physical Dot Area Equation

$$\text{Physical dot area} = 100 \times \left(\frac{1 - 10^{-\text{Tint}/n}}{1 - 10^{-\text{Solid}/n}} \right)$$

where *tint* and *solid* are the net densities.

$$
\begin{aligned}
n = \ &1.65 \ (\text{Coated paper}) \\
&2.70 \ (\text{Uncoated paper}) \\
&2.60 \ (\text{Dupont Cromalin}) \\
&4.00 \ (\text{3M Color-Key}) \\
&1.20 \ (\text{Offset plates})
\end{aligned}
$$

Net density means density minus plate density or substrate density.

$$\text{Physical dot gain} = \text{Physical dot area} - \text{Film dot area}$$

where *film dot area* is the film dot area that produced the equivalent physical dot area on the plate or substrate.

Example

Suppose a 50% plate image area and a solid plate image area yield densities of 0.41 and 1.24, respectively, then:

$$\text{Physical dot area} = 100 \times \left(\frac{1 - 10^{-0.41/1.20}}{1 - 10^{-1.24/1.20}} \right)$$

$$= 100 \times \left(\frac{1 - 10^{-0.0341666667}}{1 - 10^{-1.033333333}} \right)$$

$$= 100 \times \left(\frac{1 - 0.455337410}{1 - 0.0092611873} \right)$$

$$= 100 \times \left(\frac{0.544662590}{0.907388127} \right)$$

$$= 100 \times 0.6003$$

$$= 60.03$$

$$\approx 60\%$$

A 50% plate image area was measured, therefore:

$$\text{Physical dot gain} = 60 - 50$$

$$= 10\%$$

3 Print Contrast

If not for a number of associated problems, it would be desirable to use very high solid ink densities for printed halftones and four-color reproductions. High solid ink densities create saturated colors and dense text matter. Nevertheless, the solid ink density limit for halftones and four-color process work, even under optimal conditions, is usually reached in the 1.50 to 1.60 density range. From this point on, shadow areas will start to fill in due to the ensuing dot gain, causing a flat reproduction with no or little image detail in the shadow areas.

Print contrast measures the ratio of a shadow area density to solid ink density.

Specifically, print contrast values can be used to determine the optimal ink density for existing printing conditions and the excellence of a printed reproduction because high print contrast can generally be interpreted to mean superior print quality.

In practice, very high print contrast is achievable only under optimal printing conditions, which means well-maintained equipment capable of transferring images with the merest of impression squeeze, very stiff or tacky inks, and premium quality coated paper. These conditions and materials minimize dot gain while allowing the use of a maximum amount of ink.

As stated previously, print contrast could be used to answer the much-asked question, "At what density should a job be run?" In order to determine this, a test pressrun has to be made with incremental increases of ink flow from extremely small to extremely large amounts of ink.

The resulting print contrast, when plotted on a graph (Figure 2.3.1), will form a symmetrical curve. The curve can be explained as follows. Extremely small amounts of ink

Figure 2.3.1.
The tendency of rising and falling print contrast with increasing amounts of ink occurs in every instance, but the precise solid ink density to print contrast relationship could vary considerably depending on the printing conditions.

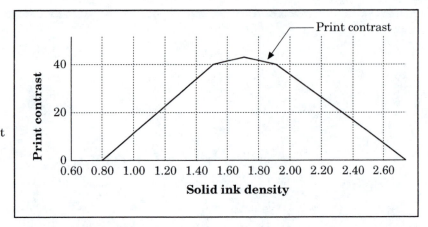

cause mottled and grayed out solid ink density image areas that are barely darker than the shadow areas. With each incremental increase of ink, the difference between solid ink density and shadow area increases, mainly because the greater amounts of ink are now creating a more completely covered and denser solid image area, while maintaining shadow dots that are still distinctly separate from each other. However, any additional amounts of ink beyond the point where maximum print contrast is achieved decreases print contrast at about the same rate it increased before maximum print contrast was reached. Beyond the point of maximum contrast, the solid ink density does not increase as fast as the shadow area, simply because the shadow area will start to fill in, diminishing the differences between solid ink densities and shadow densities until both have identical densities. At this point all shadow detail is lost and printing contrast is zero.

It goes without saying that the optimum solid ink density should be the solid ink density that produced the highest print contrast.

Print control strips should contain 75% screen patches because by convention this screen percentage is used for the purpose of print contrast measurements. A solid ink density patch should be located in the same ink zone as the 75% screen patch, preferably immediately adjacent to it.

Exact print contrast standards have not been published, but a few guidelines for different printing systems can suggest typical and approximate values (Table 2.3.1).

Print contrast is a good general indicator of print quality and it is a print quality value to which the axiom "the more the better" applies.

Table 2.3.1.
Approximate
print contrast
guidelines.

	Black	Cyan	Magenta	Yellow
Sheetfed offset	40%	36%	36%	30%
Web offset, magazines	36%	31%	31%	28%
Non-heatset web, newspapers	24%	22%	22%	18%

**Print Contrast
Equation**

Print contrast =

$$100 \times \left(\frac{\text{Solid ink density} - \text{Density of 75\% tint}}{\text{Solid ink density}} \right)$$

All measurements should be taken in close proximity to each other, preferably in the same ink zone.

Example

Suppose a 75% print control strip patch and a neighboring solid ink density patch yield densities of 0.92 and 1.32, respectively, then:

$$\text{Print contrast} = 100 \times \left(\frac{1.32 - 0.92}{1.32} \right)$$

$$= 100 \times \left(\frac{0.40}{1.32} \right)$$

$$= 100 \times 0.303$$

$$= 30.3$$

$$\approx 30\%$$

4 Ink Trap (Preucil)

Four-color process printing on multicolor presses requires each layer of ink to be superimposed over a previously printed layer of ink within time intervals as little as a fraction of a second and rarely more than a few seconds, depending on the printing speed and printing press design.

It follows that the layers of ink are still wet when meeting each other, which has the effect of the superimposed ink layer not being transferred as completely as if it were printed on a dry surface such as unprinted paper. This is an ink trapping problem, which we acknowledge as inevitable within acceptable and measurable tolerances.

Almost worse than not achieving a particular ink trap value are inconsistent ink trap values within a pressrun because the amount of ink that is trapped over a previously printed ink affects color balance profoundly and would result in inconsistent color reproductions. For example, a green created with cyan printed first and yellow printed second would cause greens to appear more or less yellowish because of the green's varying yellow content.

Ink makers are well aware of this problem and for this reason they formulate inks with different tack values. It is known that an ink lay-down sequence in which each successive ink in the sequence has a decreasing tack value improves ink trapping considerably. So-called quickset inks achieve the same effect with inks that have identical can-tack values due to their ability to dynamically increase their tack or stickiness during printing.

The definition of ink trap as measured with a densitometer is: "The ratio of a second down ink film onto a previously printed ink film minus any amount of the second-down ink that may be contained in the previously printed ink film,

Figure 2.4.1.
Graphical representation of ink trapping. In the top example, 100% of the second-down ink traps on both the paper and the first-down ink. In the bottom example, only 70% of the second-down ink traps on the first-down ink, compared to 100% on the paper.

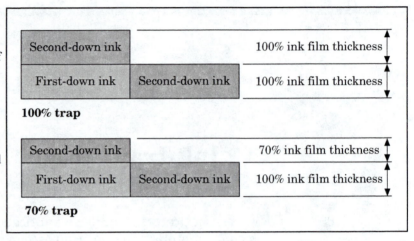

relative to the second-down ink film on white paper" (Figure 2.4.1).

Ink trap measurements are valid only with process color inks and are measured on secondary color overprint patches and their two primary color components. For example, to make ink trap measurements of a green that was created with cyan and yellow, the green, cyan, and yellow control strip patches would have to be measured. The ink lay-down sequence must be known in order to set up the formula correctly and to determine the filter value to be used. The general rule for filter values to be used is that the complementary filter for the second-down ink is used for all three values in the equation. That is, if the second-down ink is yellow, all three color patches must be measured through the blue filter; if the second-down ink is cyan, all three color patches must be measured through the red filter; and if the second-down color is magenta, all three color patches must be measured through the green filter.

In order to measure print trap, print control strips should include two-color overprint patches of green, blue, and red, as well as their respective primary color components cyan, magenta, and yellow. It is imperative for accuracy of measurements that the two primary color components of a secondary color are situated and measured in its proximity, preferably adjacent or at least in the same ink zone.

Exact print trap standards have not been published, but a few guidelines for different printing systems can suggest typical and approximate values (Table 2.4.1).

The trapping values using this mathematical approach are probably not accurate in the absolute sense, but nevertheless

Table 2.4.1.
Approximate
trap guidelines.

	Red	Green	Blue
Sheetfed offset	70%	80%	75%
Web offset, magazines	65	75	70
Non-heatset web, newspapers	55	65	60

can be valuable in maintaining consistent trap values within a pressrun and from job to job because it measures, at least relatively, that aspect of color consistency that is dependent on second-down color acceptance.

Preucil Ink Trap Equation

Ink trap = 100 ×

$$\left(\frac{\text{Density of two-color overprint} - \text{Density of first-down ink}}{\text{Density of second-down ink}} \right)$$

where density is measured through the complementary filter of the second-down ink. For example, if green is created by printing yellow on top of cyan, then all three densities are measured through the blue filter, which is the complementary filter for the second-down color, yellow. All densities are net values.

Example 1

Suppose a four-color process reproduction was printed in a CYMK sequence. The trap value of the red overprint would have to be determined using green densitometer filter values because green is the complementary color of magenta. If these green filter values are red 1.02, magenta 1.35, and yellow 0.07, then:

$$\text{Ink trap} = 100 \times \left(\frac{1.02 - 0.07}{1.35} \right)$$

$$= 100 \times \left(\frac{0.95}{1.35} \right)$$

$$= 100 \times 0.703$$

$$= 70.3$$

$$\approx 70\% \text{ of magenta ink traps on yellow to create red}$$

Example 2

Suppose a four-color process reproduction was printed in a CMYK sequence. The trap value of the green overprint would have to be determined using blue densitometer filter values, because blue is the complementary color of yellow. If these blue filter values are green 1.27, yellow 1.34, and cyan 0.20, then:

$$\text{Ink trap} = 100 \times \left(\frac{1.27 - 0.20}{1.34}\right)$$

$$= 100 \times \left(\frac{1.07}{1.34}\right)$$

$$= 100 \times 0.7985$$

$$= 79.85$$

$$\approx 80\% \text{ of yellow ink traps on cyan to create green}$$

Example 3

Suppose a four-color process reproduction was printed in a MCYK sequence. The trap value of the blue overprint would have to be determined using red densitometer filter values, because red is the complementary color of cyan. If these red filter values are blue 1.09, cyan 1.29, and magenta 0.12, then:

$$\text{Ink trap} = 100 \times \left(\frac{1.09 - 0.12}{1.29}\right)$$

$$= 100 \times \left(\frac{0.97}{1.29}\right)$$

$$= 100 \times 0.7519$$

$$= 75.19$$

$$\approx 75\% \text{ cyan ink traps on magenta to create blue}$$

5   Ink Trap (Brunner)

What Is the Difference Between the Brunner and Preucil Ink Trap Equations?

The Brunner print trap method addresses the issue of print trap in a similar way as the Preucil method in that all values used in the equation are derived from densitometer filter values of the second-down ink, but the similarities end here.

First, in the Brunner equation all densities are converted to their equivalent light absorption values, while in the Preucil equation all densities remain unconverted.

Second, Brunner chooses to add the second-down color content of the first-down ink to the second-down ink printed on paper, while Preucil chooses to subtract the second-down color content of the first-down ink from the second-down color content of the overprint. This is also the reason why the Brunner equation typically yields much higher printing trap values between 80% and 99%, with the 95% to 99% range being considered ideal.

The Brunner printing trap equation is the ratio of a second-down ink onto a previously printed ink, relative to the sum of the second-down ink on white paper and the second-down color content of the first-down ink.

These are important differences and the jury is still out in determining which equation is more accurate when measuring the actual or absolute amounts of ink that are trapped when two wet inks are superimposed over each other. Ultimately, the benefit of both methods is not their absolute accuracy, but their ability to monitor relative changes of the amount of ink transferred when printing wet on wet ink films, a task that both equations accomplish adequately.

The Brunner ink trap equation is relatively uncommon in North America and is discussed here in the interest of comprehensiveness.

**Brunner
Ink Trap
Equation**

Ink trap =

$$100 \times \left(\frac{1 - 10^{-\text{Density of two-color overprint}}}{1 - 10^{-(\text{Density of second-down ink + density of first-down ink})}} \right)$$

where density is measured through the complementary filter of the second-down ink, i.e., if green is created by printing yellow on top of cyan, then all three densities are measured through the blue filter, which is the complimentary filter for the second-down color yellow. All densities are net values.

Example

Suppose a four-color process reproduction was printed in a CYMK sequence. The trap value of the red overprint would have to be determined using green densitometer filter values because green is the complementary color of magenta. If these green filter values are red 1.02, magenta 1.35, and yellow 0.07, then:

$$\text{Ink trap} = 100 \times \left(\frac{1 - 10^{-1.02}}{1 - 10^{-(1.35 + 0.07)}} \right)$$

$$= 100 \times \left(\frac{1 - 10^{-1.02}}{1 - 10^{-1.42}} \right)$$

$$= 100 \times \left(\frac{1 - 0.095499259}{1 - 0.038018940} \right)$$

$$= 100 \times \left(\frac{0.904500741}{0.961981060} \right)$$

$$= 100 \times 0.940247972$$

$$= 94.02$$

$$\approx 94\% \text{ magenta ink traps on yellow to create red}$$

Values in this problem are identical to those in example 1 of the preceding Preucil ink trap calculations. Please note the higher ink trap values from the Brunner equation.

6   Hue Error and Grayness

In theory, cyan, yellow, and magenta printing inks in combination with each other should be able to reproduce an infinite number of colors, or by logical extension any color that may exist in an original copy to be printed. The underlying reasoning is their theoretical and combined capacity to reflect all wavelengths in the visible spectrum. A theoretically pure cyan absorbs exactly one-third of the spectrum, namely the red portions, and reflects the rest of the spectrum consisting of the blue and green portions. Likewise, a pure magenta absorbs green while reflecting red and blue, and a pure yellow absorbs all blue while the red and green portions of the spectrum are reflected in their entirety. If, for example, all three of these process colors were superimposed over each other, they each should absorb their respective third of the spectrum resulting in total light absorption and therefore a perfect black (Figure 2.6.1A–C).

In practice we know this is not the case, because the superimposition of all three process colors creates a color resembling brown rather than black. This can be explained by the fact that real physical process inks do not reflect all of the light waves they are supposed to reflect. Also, some process colors reflect the desirable light waves unequally. Moreover, all process color inks reflect some light waves in the third of the spectrum that should be absorbed entirely.

Specifically, cyan absorbs large portions of the blue and green spectrum, magenta reflects much more red than blue, and yellow has no appreciable reflective deficiencies, which is why cyan inks are known to be too grayish, magenta inks too reddish, and yellow inks as the purest of the set (Figure 2.6.2A–C).

The natural limitations of ink pigments and their manufacture impose these imperfections, and it is in part the

Figure 2.6.1A.
Spectral reflectance curve of a "perfect" cyan ink.

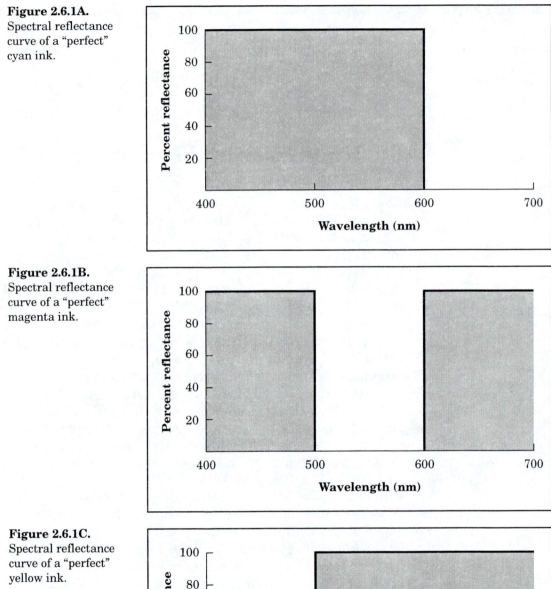

Figure 2.6.1B.
Spectral reflectance curve of a "perfect" magenta ink.

Figure 2.6.1C.
Spectral reflectance curve of a "perfect" yellow ink.

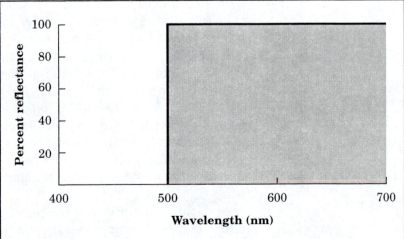

Figure 2.6.2A.
Spectral reflectance
of a typical cyan ink.

Figure 2.6.2B.
Spectral reflectance
curve of a typical
magenta ink.

Figure 2.6.2C.
Spectral reflectance
curve of a typical yel-
low ink.

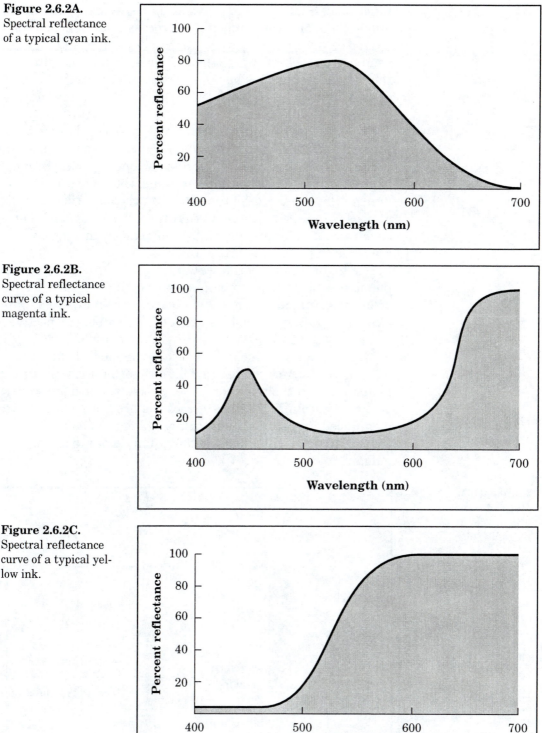

function of hue error and grayness measurements to control and standardize these inevitable process color deficiencies.

Hue error and grayness values are derived from reading each process color through the red, green, and blue filters of the densitometer. This has the effect of measuring the approximate reflectance of each process color across the entire visible spectrum.

From the previous discussion it was learned that each process color absorbs one-third and reflects two-thirds of the spectrum and that real process inks are not perfect. Because of process inks' inherent imperfections, they will absorb some light in the two-thirds of the spectrum they are theoretically supposed to reflect. It follows that the relative densities of each process color are one high filter reading and two filter readings that are not quite zero.

The highest density is always measured through the complementary filter of the nominal color being measured. Thus, cyan, magenta, and yellow will always have red-, green-, and blue-filter values as their highest density values, respectively.

Usually the three filter values will consist of a high, medium, and low value in which case the medium value determines hue error (Figure 2.6.3). If both minor values are identical, then the hue error is zero because the equal contribution of both minor values causes the process color to have a balanced hue, i.e., a yellow can be thought of as being contaminated with minuscule but equal amounts of cyan and magenta.

Figure 2.6.3.
Hue error and grayness of a magenta ink.

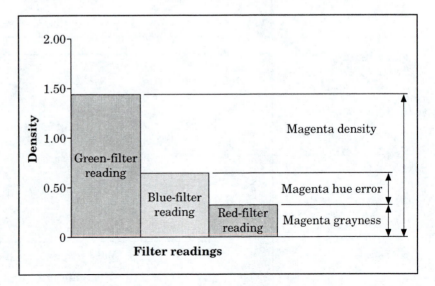

Grayness is a function of the lowest value, because the lowest color content, combined with equal amounts of the two colors contained in the medium and high density values, will create a gray factor that tends to dull or desaturate the nominal color (Figure 2.6.3).

Finally, ink efficiency is a measure of the two undesirable absorptions in relation to the desirable absorption expressed as a percentage ratio. A 100% efficiency would mean that both minor values are zero, while 0% efficiency would mean that the sum of both are twice as much as the major or highest value. Efficiency is useful as an index of total color deficiency but is not suitable to identify the contributing factors, hue error and grayness, individually.

Exact hue error and grayness standards have not been published, but a few guidelines for different printing systems can suggest typical and approximate values (Table 2.6.1).

Table 2.6.1.
Approximate guidelines for hue error and grayness.

	Cyan	Magenta	Yellow
Sheetfed offset	Hue: 20 Gray: 14	Hue: 46 Gray: 14	Hue: 5 Gray: 6
Web offset, magazines	Hue: 21 Gray: 21	Hue: 50 Gray: 18	Hue: 6 Gray: 15
Nonheatset, newspapers	Hue: 28 Gray: 42	Hue: 56 Gray: 34	Hue: 10 Gray: 25

Hue Error, Grayness, and Efficiency Equations

$$\text{Hue error} = 100 \times \left(\frac{\text{Mid density} - \text{Low density}}{\text{High density} - \text{Low density}} \right)$$

$$\text{Grayness} = 100 \times \left(\frac{\text{Low density}}{\text{High density}} \right)$$

$$\text{Efficiency} = 100 - \left(\frac{(\text{Mid density} + \text{Low density}) \times 100}{2 \times \text{High density}} \right)$$

Examples

Suppose a solid cyan ink patch yields red, blue, and green densitometer filter readings of 1.30, 0.39, and 0.14, respectively, then:

$$\text{Hue error} = 100 \times \left(\frac{0.39 - 0.14}{1.30 - 0.14} \right)$$

$$= 100 \times \left(\frac{0.25}{1.16} \right)$$

$$= 100 \times 0.2155$$

$$= 21.55$$

$$\approx 22\%$$

$$\text{Grayness} = 100 \times \left(\frac{0.14}{1.30} \right)$$

$$= 100 \times 0.1076$$

$$= 10.76$$

$$\approx 11\%$$

$$\text{Efficiency} = 100 - \left(\frac{(0.39 + 0.14) \times 100}{2 \times 1.30} \right)$$

$$= 100 - \left(\frac{0.53 \times 100}{2.60} \right)$$

$$= 100 - \left(\frac{53}{2.60} \right)$$

$$= 100 - 20.384615$$

$$= 79.615$$

$$\approx 80\%$$

7 Density

The reproduction of printed images, in particular during the printing phase, is susceptible to tonal and color variations primarily because of the dot size (described in section 1), ink trap (described in section 2), and ink film thickness.

The latter reason, ink film thickness, is usually measured instrumentally with a densitometer and is expressed as a unit of measurement called density, which is the abbreviated term for optical density.

For better understanding of this topic a brief discussion of color dimensions is useful.

A complete description of a color is possible only when its three dimensions, hue, chroma, and value, are quantified. Hue is simply the nominal designation of the color; for example, green as opposed to red. Chroma is the purity or saturation of the color, and value is the lightness or darkness of the color.

Ink film thickness variations affect all of these color dimensions, yet densitometers are not specifically designed to measure them. Nevertheless, as shall be seen later in this section, densitometers have a useful purpose in aiming for and maintaining consistency of tonal values and color during printing production.

The perception of color from a printed layer of process ink is caused by the interaction of incident light and the resonance of certain pigments to certain of the light's wavelengths. As the light travels through the ink film, some wavelengths are absorbed selectively by the ink's pigments. Eventually, the non-absorbed wavelengths reach the usually white substrate that reflects it back through the ink film to the eyes of an observer whose perceptual system processes the light stimulation as a color such as magenta.

With small amounts of ink or thin ink films, the chroma of the resulting color tends to be low, or in other words the color will appear dull. Incremental increases of ink film thickness will see the color's chroma intensify continuously, because more pigments accumulate in the thicker ink film.

Beyond certain ink film thickness, however, the color changes visibly, as any press operator who inadvertently overinked during the early stages of a makeready knows. Magenta could change to a maroon, and a cyan could turn into a dark blue. This hue change is caused by an over-abundance of pigments in the excessively thick ink film.

Also contributing to this color transformation is the color's changing value because, with increased ink film thickness, less light reaches the white substrate surface, causing the color to appear increasingly dark.

It becomes abundantly clear that the achievement of color fidelity in printing production is highly dependent on ink film thickness, and that if ink film thickness could be measured, color could be controlled.

It is generally accepted that ink film thicknesses ranging from 0.7 to 1.1 μm are necessary to produce true process colors in the offset lithographic process (1 μm = $\frac{1}{1,000}$ mm).

A densitometer's measuring principle is based on a stabilized light source that is projected through lenses and filters onto a colored surface, which absorbs the light more or less depending on the thickness of the ink film. Thick ink films will naturally absorb more light than thin ink films. The non-absorbed reflected portions of light are captured by a photodiode that measures its electrical energy. The electrical energy is compared to a reference value for an absolute white and the difference is mathematically converted to an optical density.

Thus it can be stated that densities are a measure of light absorbed by a colored surface and that ink film thickness, while not specifically measured by a densitometer, can be extrapolated.

Tests have shown that an approximate linear correlation exists between densities and ink film thickness, especially in the density range that is relevant for printing (Figure 2.7.1). This validates the densitometer as a means to measure and monitor the print characteristic that is largely responsible for tonal values and color fidelity.

Figure 2.7.1.
Ink film thickness–
density relationship.

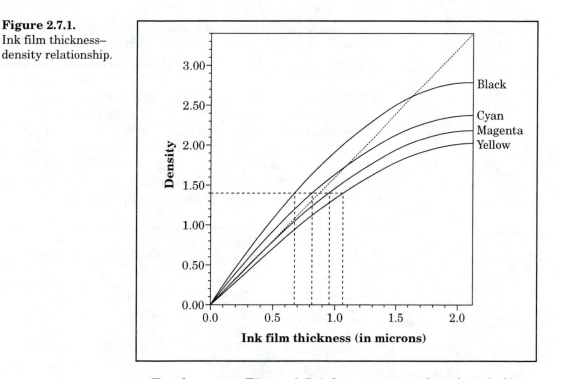

Furthermore, Figure 2.7.1 demonstrates that the ink film thickness for each process color is not exactly the same for a given density. The actual ink film thickness–density relationship may vary from one process color set to the other, and it must be considered when calibrating computerized scanning densitometers that are interfaced with the ink feed system of a press. Without this compensation the system will "assume" that the amounts of ink necessary to make automatic corrections are identical for all colors, which is usually not the case.

In practice, color control with a densitometer becomes a matter of calibrating the instrument to the manufacturer's standard and then aiming for densities that are either visually acceptable or are known to produce good tonal definition and color balance in four-color process printing.

Henceforth, these density values are monitored during the pressrun within acceptable and achievable tolerances, with ±0.05 being close to the lower limit for achievable tolerances from an aimpoint. This approach to printing production assures not only good and consistent quality but also increases productivity because the process is guided by concrete quality standards that are not dependent on potentially time-consuming, wasteful, and subjective evaluation.

The density equation is the logarithm of the ratio of the absorbed light of an absolute white to the light absorbed by a measured ink film. The reason why densities are expressed as logarithmic numbers is related to the visual response of the human eye to radiant energy. The human eye perceives increasing amounts of light in an approximate logarithmic progression; that is, for every doubling of radiant energy received, the observer's perceptual system experiences only one-tenth the amount. This is apparent from Table 2.7.1, when comparing the 10% and 1% reflection values and their corresponding densities of 1.00 and 2.00, respectively.

Table 2.7.1.
Reflectance, opacity, and density.

Reflectance	Percent Reflectance	Opacity	Density
1.000	100.00	1.000	0.00
0.794	79.43	1.259	0.10
0.631	63.10	1.585	0.20
0.501	50.12	1.995	0.30
0.398	39.81	2.512	0.40
0.316	31.62	3.162	0.50
0.251	25.12	3.981	0.60
0.199	19.95	5.012	0.70
0.158	15.85	6.310	0.80
0.126	12.59	7.943	0.90
0.100	10.000	10.000	1.00
0.079	7.943	12.59	1.10
0.063	6.310	15.85	1.20
0.050	5.012	19.95	1.30
0.040	3.981	25.12	1.40
0.032	3.162	31.62	1.50
0.025	2.512	39.81	1.60
0.020	1.995	50.12	1.70
0.016	1.585	63.10	1.80
0.013	1.259	79.43	1.90
0.010	1.000	100.00	2.00

The densitometer is for these reasons an indispensable tool for controlling the printing process related factor of ink film thickness, which is largely responsible for color and tonal values. Furthermore, the density scale approximates the visual response of the human eye.

Dry ink films usually have lower densities than wet ink films due to a phenomenon called dry-back. Light reflects from wet ink films in a specular or mirror-like fashion, while dry ink films, having conformed to the irregularities of the substrate, reflect light in a diffused or scattered manner, which causes the densitometer's photodiode to receive more light. Densitometers equipped with polarization filters read wet and dry ink films more nearly the same. Polarization filters eliminate specular reflection or light reflected from the surface of measured samples and therefore sends less light to the receiver. This fact accounts for the lower densities obtained from densitometers with polarization filters for both dry and wet ink films.

The filters, through which each process color is measured, are the visual, red, green, and blue filters for black, cyan, magenta, and yellow, respectively. Note that the filters used for the chromatic colors cyan, magenta, and yellow are their complementary color or the color that should be absorbed. This relates to the fact that correlation between the reflected complementary colors of process inks and ink film thickness is particularly good.

Exact recommendations for optimum solid ink densities cannot be made with a high degree of accuracy because of the almost infinite paper and ink combinations used in the printing industry. These widely varying printing conditions require different densities in order to produce acceptable print quality. The following guidelines (Table 2.7.2) for solid ink densities must be seen in this light and are more useful for their comparative than their absolute values.

Table 2.7.2.
Approximate guidelines for densities, using a Status-T densitometer.

	Black	Cyan	Magenta	Yellow
Sheetfed offset*	1.70	1.40	1.50	1.10
Web offset, magazines*	1.55	1.30	1.40	1.00
Nonheatset, newspapers*	1.05	0.90	0.90	0.85

*Sheetfed offset and web offset printing on coated papers; nonheatset printing on newsprint.

Optical Density Equation

$$\text{Density} = \text{Log}_{10}\frac{1}{\text{ß}}$$

$$\text{where ß} = \frac{\text{Light reflectance of the printed ink film}}{\text{Light reflectance of a reference white}}$$

Example

Suppose the ratio of light reflected from a printed ink film and a reference white is 0.07943, then:

$$\text{Density} = \text{Log}_{10}\frac{1}{0.07943}$$

$$= \text{Log}_{10}\ 12.58970162$$

$$= 1.100015437$$

$$\approx 1.10$$

The result can be verified in Table 2.7.1.

8   Reflectance/Opacity

Fundamentally, densities are mathematically derived from light reflection. The reason why densities rather than reflected light percentages are used in quantifying the relative darkness of a printed copy is because the density scale, being based on logarithmic numbers, approaches the human eye's sensitivity to light stimulation more nearly the same. (For more information on this topic refer to section 7).

While there is no practical application for reflectance values in the day-to-day operation of a printing company, knowledge of density and reflectance interrelationships facilitates an understanding of densitometry in general.

Related print characteristics such as dot area measurements, Brunner ink trap, and ink absorption use variations of the reflectance value calculations in their equations.

Opacity means the ability of a material to prevent light from passing through it and is the reciprocal of reflectance. Similar to the density scale, opacity increases by a factor of 10 for every halving of the amount of light reflected.

To calculate light reflectance from a density value, base 10 is raised to the negative exponent density. To calculate opacity from a density value, base 10 is raised to the positive exponent density.

Reflectance and Opacity Equations

$$\text{Light reflectance} = 10^{-\text{Density}}$$

$$\text{Opacity} = 10^{\text{Density}}$$

Example 1

Suppose a cyan solid ink density yields a density of 1.50, then:

$$\text{Reflection} = 10^{-1.50}$$

$$= 0.031622777$$

$$\approx 0.032$$

$$\text{Opacity} = 10^{1.50}$$

$$= 31.62277660$$

$$\approx 31.62$$

Example 2   Opacity is the reciprocal of reflection; therefore, a reflectance value of 0.020 converts to:

$$\text{Opacity} = \frac{1}{0.020}$$

$$= 50.00$$

The results can be verified in Table 2.7.1.

9   Ink Absorption of Paper

All conventional printing processes require a liquid coloring agent in order for the reproduced images to come alive on paper or other types of substrate. This coloring agent is called printing ink, which could be as fluid as water or as viscous as lard, depending on the printing process used.

The printing inks used in the offset lithographic process fall in the more viscous category and for that reason are sometimes called paste inks. Viscous as they may be, these paste inks are equally subject to many of the principles of kinetic theory, as are other more fluid liquids.

Conventional printing processes, in essence, apply printing ink onto a substrate such as paper using pressure. Given these circumstances and the fact that paper is a more or less porous material, it is to be expected that some of the ink will be absorbed into its inner fiber structure.

The absorption of ink into paper is both a necessity and quality detraction.

Some degree of ink absorption is necessary, as otherwise ink smearing and ink setoff are likely to occur. Ink absorption's quality detraction stems from a loss of the ink's chromatic properties, due to its partial dispersion into the paper's interior.

Papers that absorb large amounts of ink are said to have low ink holdout or thin ink films on the surface of the paper. Conversely, papers with low ink absorbency have high ink holdout or thick ink films on the surface of the paper.

In general, uncoated papers and newsprint have low ink holdout, and consequently their achievable print quality with respect to color saturation does not rate as high as coated papers, which have higher ink holdout.

The problem of ink setoff, referred to earlier, is not as much an issue with uncoated papers because of their relatively low ink holdout. Coated papers, on the other hand, are very susceptible to ink setoff, specifically because of their relatively high ink holdout. For this reason coated papers almost always require spraying with antisetoff powder, which effectively forms a barrier between all sheets as they are deposited on the delivery pile.

The test for ink absorption described here requires a special testing ink called K and N ink, as well as a densitometer.

A small amount of the testing ink is applied to overlapping samples of different papers, using a drawdown blade, and is left to be absorbed into the papers for two minutes. The excess ink is then wiped off with a soft cloth. This procedure produces stains with varying intensities on each paper. The darker the stain, the more absorbent the paper.

If the objective of the test is to rank the papers according to their absorbency, then their relative darkness is measured with a densitometer and the lowest to highest absorbency would correspond with lowest and highest densities, respectively.

If absolute amounts of absorptions are required, the K and N ink stain densities can be converted into ink absorption percentages directly from a conversion chart, such as shown in Figure 2.9.1, or by mathematical conversion.

Figure 2.9.1.
Ink absorption of paper chart.

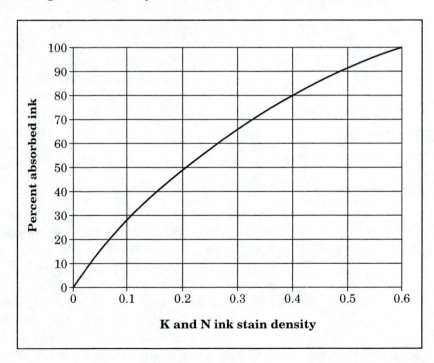

The definition of the ink absorption equation is "the density of a stain produced by a special testing ink and procedure, which is a function of the percentage of voids and capillaries in the interior of paper that are saturated with this ink. Where zero density means zero absorption and 0.60 density means 100% absorption."

K and N
Ink Absorption
of Paper
Equation

$$\text{K and N ink absorption} =$$
$$1.333 \times (100 - \text{Percentage of light reflectance})$$

where *light reflectance* is the light reflectance from a K and N test stain.

Note: The gray K and N test ink was formulated to produce a maximum density of 0.60, at which point 100% absorption is reached.

Example

Suppose a K and N test stain yields a density of 0.30, then:

$$\% \text{ light reflectance from K and N ink stain} = 10^{-0.30} \times 100$$

$$= 0.501187234 \times 100$$

$$= 50.11872336$$

$$\approx 50\%$$

$$\text{K and N ink absorption of paper} = 1.333 \times (100 - 50)$$

$$= 1.333 \times 50$$

$$= 66.5$$

$$\approx 67\%$$

10 Paper Surface Efficiency

Printers know by experience that papers with nearly identical visual characteristics do not necessarily assure repeatability of print attributes such as hue and grayness. Likewise, it is not unusual for papers with different visual characteristics to produce very similar print results. The problem becomes one of objective selection of papers, since a paper's visual characteristics are not a reliable predictor of print quality.

The two paper properties that have a major effect on this discrepancy between paper appearance and expected print quality are a paper's capacity to absorb ink (described in section 9) and paper gloss.

Paper gloss is imparted on paper by surface treatments such as various coating methods and calendering, all of which increase the paper surface smoothness, causing incident light to be reflected in spectral or mirror-like fashion. Paper gloss is measured with a photo reflection or gloss meter on a scale from 0 to 100. High gloss papers will tend to reflect printed surfaces with greater intensity, resulting in more saturated colors and increased color gamut.

The general concept of paper surface efficiency (PSE) is based on the fact that each of these two paper properties has an equal and opposite effect on print quality. This means that if both properties are measured on a scale from 0% to 100%, then 0% ink absorption has the exact same effect on print quality as 100% paper gloss.

The explanation for the PSE rationale is quite logical, because high amounts of ink absorbed into the interior of the paper structure will diminish an ink's chromatic saturation in the same way and magnitude as reduced light reflection from the surface of the paper due to low gloss.

The apparent contradiction of visually dissimilar papers producing similar print results can now be explained by the PSE principle. A given paper with high gloss and high ink absorption will be visibly different from another paper that has low gloss and low ink absorption. What the former paper gains in color saturation from high paper gloss and loses from high ink absorption, the latter paper inversely proportionally loses from low paper gloss and gains from low absorption.

In practice, PSE can be used to monitor incoming raw materials. If the measured PSE of new deliveries of paper from different lots remains consistent, production quality is also more likely to stay stable.

PSE values are usually much higher for coated than for uncoated papers, but rarely exceed 70%. Non-fibrous metal and synthetic substrates, however, can reach PSE values of close to 90% and are known to surpass paper in its ability to reproduce highly saturated colors.

Figure 2.10.1.
Paper surface efficiency.

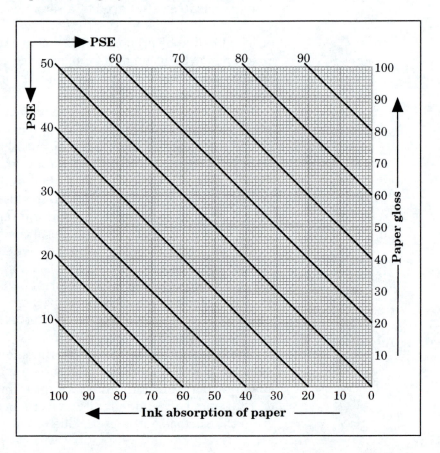

PSE can be determined directly from a conversion chart, such as that shown in Figure 2.10.1, or by mathematical conversion.

The PSE equation is the average of paper gloss and the inverse of paper ink absorption.

PSE Equation

$$\text{PSE} = \frac{(100 - \text{Ink absorption of paper}) + \text{Gloss}}{2}$$

If a paper has an ink absorption value of 40% and a gloss value of 60%, then:

$$\text{PSE} = \frac{(100 - 40) + 60}{2}$$

$$= \frac{60 + 60}{2}$$

$$= \frac{120}{2}$$

$$= 60$$

Example 2

If a paper has an ink absorption value of 60% and a gloss value of 80%, then:

$$\text{PSE} = \frac{(100 - 60) + 80}{2}$$

$$= \frac{40 + 80}{2}$$

$$= \frac{120}{2}$$

$$= 60$$

Please note that two papers with different ink absorption and gloss values can yield identical PSE values.

11　Printing Cylinder Calculations

Image Length Change

Paper, along with the images on it, has a propensity to change its size when exposed to varying atmospheric conditions. (For further information on paper's dimensional stability, refer to part 1, section 8.) The dimensional changes are miniscule and, as such, are generally imperceptible as a change of overall image or paper size; yet they are significant when colors are printed in multiple pressruns, causing images to fit imprecisely onto previously printed images by reason of their changed size.

Dimensional changes are known to be greater in the cross grain direction of paper. Therefore, a favorable grain direction orientation, together with an image manipulation technique involving packing sheet shifts between blanket and plate cylinder, can be used to solve image fit problems.

The term packing denotes the adjustment of plate and blanket heights relative to the cylinder bearers in order to print with correct pressure or impression "squeeze" usually attained in the vicinity of 0.003–0.006 in. To assure a correct impression squeeze and equal surface speeds of both cylinders, packing of plates and blankets is normally done according to the press manufacturer's specifications.

Because the surface speed of cylinders is fundamentally related to image length, one must apply the principles of image length manipulation purposefully. In order for image dimensions to be reproduced in true length in the circumferential direction of the printing cylinders, the blanket and plate cylinders must travel equally fast at their surfaces. Equal speed at the cylinder centers and bearers is assured by virtue of the cylinders being in mesh with gears, but they could travel at slightly different speeds at their surfaces, owing to the blanket's compressibility. Equal surface speeds can only occur when both cylinders are packed in such a way that their diameters at the point of contact are identical.

Owing to the requisite 0.003–0.006 in. impression squeeze, a blanket bulge on both sides of the point of contact effectively increases the blanket cylinder diameter relative to the plate cylinder. To compensate for this increase in diameter, most press manufacturers recommend packing the plate a few thousandths of an inch higher and the blanket a few thousandths of an inch lower than their respective bearers. This packing method is commonly called true rolling because both cylinders travel at identical surface speeds, producing a minimum of friction between the cylinders and true image length (Figure 2.11.1).

Figure 2.11.1.
True rolling packing method.

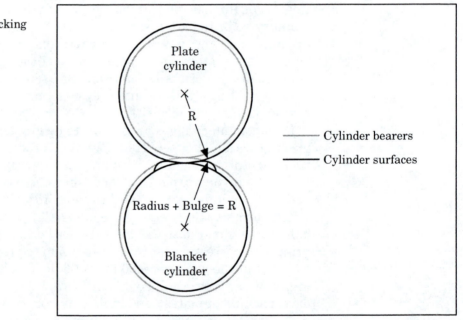

Any shift of packing from one cylinder to the other has the effect of one cylinder traveling faster than the other at the surface because a change of diameter naturally also changes its circumference, thus necessitating different distances traveled by each cylinder per revolution.

It is ultimately the blanket cylinder's diameter that governs the size of the image in the circumferential cylinder direction because it is here that the final image is created before being transferred to the paper. In other words, whatever the size of the image on the blanket is its size on the paper. If, for instance, a packing sheet is shifted from the plate to the blanket, the circumference of the blanket increases, resulting in increased image length. The opposite is true when a shift from the blanket to the plate occurs.

It will be noted that any packing change of one cylinder must necessarily be accompanied by an equal and opposite change of the other cylinder; otherwise, the correct impression squeeze could not be maintained.

The simple rule for image length change is that a shift of packing to the blanket cylinder increases image length and a shift of packing from the blanket cylinder decreases image length.

An undesirable consequence of image length change is unequal surface speeds, which cause excessive friction and, possibly, premature plate wear. For this reason, packing shifts should not be made beyond certain limits. The permissible packing shifts depend on the printing cylinder diameter and should not be exceeded. Similarly, new jobs should always be started using normal packing specifications, and packing shifts should be made only when critical image fits cannot be achieved by any other means.

Since image length changes are only possible in one cylinder direction, the paper's cross grain direction, which is subject to the greatest dimensional change, must be oriented in the circumferential direction of the printing cylinders. This means that only grain long paper benefits from the image length change procedure on presses that feed the long edge of the paper parallel to the printing cylinder axis, as is the case with the majority of medium to large sheetfed presses.

Fundamentally, image length changes are determined using the mathematical method to calculate a circle's circumference, reduced proportionally by the ratio of the measured image length to the circumference of the printing cylinder.

Image Length Change Equation

$$ILC = 2 \times \text{Packing sheet change} \times \pi \times C$$

where *ILC* is the image length change, *C* is the ratio of the image length to the printing cylinder circumference, and π is 3.141592654. The packing sheet change is measured in thousandths of an inch. (Note: the multiplier 2 is used to account for the fact that, for every packing sheet change, the diameter of the cylinder changes by an amount that is twice as much as the thickness of the packing sheet.)

Example

A special color image measuring 29.5 in. in the circumferential direction of the plate cylinder, with critical image fit requirements, is printed on a previously printed four-color process image. The image fit is being adjusted by shifting a 0.003-in. packing sheet from the plate cylinder to the blanket cylinder, each having a diameter of 13.75 in. The image length change and new image length are:

$$\text{Printing cylinder circumference} = 13.75 \times 3.141592654$$

$$= 43.19689899$$

$$\text{Ratio of image length to printing cylinder circumference} = \frac{29.5}{43.19689899}$$

$$= 0.682919392$$

$$\text{Image length change} = 2 \times 0.003 \times 3.141592654 \times 0.682919392$$

$$= 0.012872727$$

$$\approx 0.013$$

Since a packing sheet was shifted from the plate cylinder to the blanket cylinder, image length increased; therefore:

$$\text{New image length} = 29.5 + 0.013$$

$$= 29.513 \text{ in.}$$

Impression Squeeze

It is for good reason that offset printing machines are called presses. They require pressure to transfer ink from the printing plate to the blanket and again when the inked image on the blanket is transferred to the paper.

The pressure required to make these image transfers is called impression squeeze and must be calculated within a few thousandths of an inch, because an insufficient impression squeeze results in faint image quality, while an excessive impression squeeze causes images to be too dark due to a phenomenon called dot gain (for further information on dot gain, refer to sections 1 and 2).

Most modern sheetfed presses are of the bearer contact variety, which is to say that the plate and blanket cylinders rotate against each other on hardened steel rings called bearers (Figure 2.11.2). Plate and blanket cylinders, as their names imply, accommodate the printing plate and blanket, respectively, which necessitates an area called the undercut. An understanding of the term undercut is crucial to calculating impression squeeze and can be defined as the distance of the cylinder body to the surface of its respective bearer (Figure 2.11.2).

Figure 2.11.2.
Printing cylinder components.

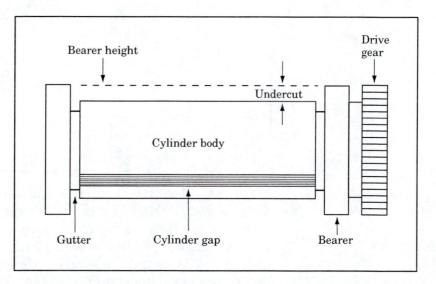

The blanket cylinder's undercut is always larger than the plate cylinder's undercut because blankets are typically much thicker than plates. In addition, the blanket and plate cylinder undercuts are larger than their respective blanket and plate because blankets and plates require underlay sheets, called packing sheets, to compensate for different blanket and plate thicknesses, to bring blankets and plates to their proper height, and to manipulate image length.

Adjusting the height of the blanket and plate relative to their respective bearers is the determining factor for the printing pressure or impression squeeze used. It could range from 0.003 in. for new and well-maintained presses to 0.006 in. for older presses.

Determining the impression squeeze involves the calculation of two sums: the total thickness of the plate and its packing and the blanket and its packing; and the combined undercuts of plate and blanket cylinders (Figure 2.11.3). Subtracting the latter sum from the former sum results in the impression squeeze.

Figure 2.11.3.
Combined undercut of plate and blanket cylinders.

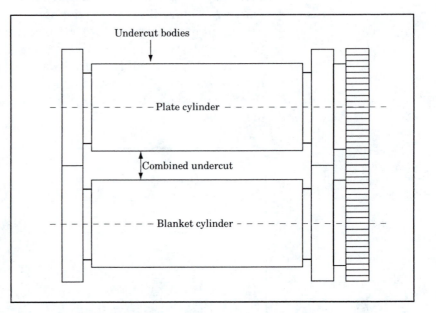

For example, if the blanket thickness is 0.080 in., the packing under the blanket is 0.012 in., the plate thickness is 0.009 in., and the packing under the plate is 0.004 in. The sum of these is 0.105 in. Furthermore, if the plate cylinder undercut is 0.010 and the blanket cylinder undercut is 0.092 in., the combined undercut is 0.102 in. Subtracting the combined undercut (0.102) from the sum of thicknesses on the plate and blanket cylinders (0.105) results in an impression squeeze of 0.003 in.

Impression
Squeeze Equation

Impression squeeze = (Blanket + Packing + Plate + Packing)
    – (Plate cylinder undercut + Blanket cylinder undercut)

Example

If the blanket thickness is 0.077 in., the blanket packing is 0.012 in., the plate thickness is 0.012 in., the plate packing is 0.006 in., the plate cylinder undercut is 0.012 in., and the blanket cylinder undercut is 0.092 in., then the impression squeeze is:

Impression squeeze =

$$(0.077 + 0.012 + 0.012 + 0.006) - (0.012 + 0.092)$$

$$= 0.107 - 0.104$$

$$= 0.003 \text{ in.}$$

12   Color Difference

The densitometer has been and probably will continue to be an effective tool for color assessment and control, albeit its usefulness is essentially limited to process colors.

The densitometer's ultimate objective of measuring ink film thickness accurately depends on the fact that process inks are manufactured according to standards that define their spectral qualities, which in turn are compatible with the densitometer filters through which light absorption is measured.

Each of the densitometer filters samples a relatively narrow range of colors encompassing an approximate band that is complementary to the process color being measured. (For further information on densitometry, refer to section 6).

These standardized conditions that permit the measurement and control of four-color processes work adequately for all quality levels.

When, however, densitometers are used to measure non-process colors, their effectiveness diminishes considerably because their filter bands do not correspond with the spectral quality of non-process colors. The filter that returns the highest reading is the best option, but this practice is far from accurate because the narrow bands of densitometer filters may not account for large spectral portions of non-process colors.

In recent years, spectrophotometers have become a viable alternative to densitometers because advances made in electronic and digital technology have reduced their size and cost. Equally important is the recent development of computer programs that can convert spectral data into printing press ink-feed values, thus permitting spectrophotometers to be connected to printing presses measuring their output and controlling ink flow.

Spectrophotometers, unlike densitometers, require no filters to measure the light re-emitted from colored surfaces, but instead employ a diffraction grating and sensors that measure the intensity of light re-emitted from a printed ink film in all parts of the visible spectrum. Because spectrophotometers sample the entire visible spectrum band from approximately 380 to 780 nanometers, they provide the most accurate and complete color information possible, regardless of its hue.

The perception of color depends on three factors, one of which is the aforementioned spectral reflectance of a colored surface. The other two equally weighty factors are the illuminant under which the colored surface is viewed and the standard observer, which is the spectral response of what can be considered normal color vision. Detailed spectral data of various illuminants exist; the so-called D50 illuminant approaches normal daylight and has therefore been selected as the standard illuminant in the graphic communications industry. The standard observer has been defined empirically by the international standard organization CIE (Commission Internationale de l'Éclairage), again resulting in detailed spectral information. Finally, tristimulus values X, Y, and Z are calculated from the spectral data of the measured color, illuminant, and standard observer by integration and multiplication. Calculating tristimulus values manually would be a tedious task because it involves large numbers of infinitesimal values that are in practice performed by hardware-integrated computer programs.

A number of color measurement systems such as CIE Y, x, y color space, CIE-UCS color space, HUNTER L,a,b color space, CIELUV color space, CIELAB color space, and Munsell H, C, V color space have been developed. The underlying commonality of these color spaces rests with their derivation from tristimulus values X, Y, and Z.

In the early 20th century, the American color theorist Munsell discovered that a complete description of color is only possible by quantifying its three qualities—hue, chroma, and value. Hue denotes the name of a color such as cyan as opposed to yellow, chroma denotes the purity or saturation, and value denotes the lightness or darkness of the color.

Since color has three qualities, it can be represented in three-dimensional spaces; thus, the term color dimension was coined. In principle, all color spaces adhere to these concepts and differ only in shape. The color spaces have amorphous shapes, reflecting the fact that a color's dimensions have unequal ranges of chroma and value depending on its hue. Graphic representation of color, however, is mostly represented by symmetrical shapes, such as spheres or cubes, ignoring the color spaces' extremities, which are normally not reproducible with physical colorants such as printing inks.

All color spaces represent a color's value on a vertical axis, with the uppermost extremity denoting white and the lowermost extremity denoting black. The chroma is represented by a horizontal axis that denotes maximum chroma or saturation at the periphery of the color space and minimum saturation or total desaturation (i.e., black, a shade of gray, or white) at the center of the color space.

The preferred chromaticity systems in today's graphic communications industry are the CIELAB and CIELUV color spaces because of their relatively good approximation of the human eye's sensitivity to color stimulation. In principle, both of these color spaces are identical and differ only in shapes; therefore, all further discussion will be focussed on the CIELAB color space.

The CIELAB color space represents the color dimensions using notations L^*, a^*, b^*, where L^* signifies a color's value. An L^* value of 100, 50, and 0 that traverses the center of the color space means white, gray, and black, respectively. The hue and chroma dimensions are represented by notations a^* and b^*, where $-b^*$ = blue, b^* = yellow, $-a^*$ = green, and a^* = red. This type of color space is sometimes also called opponent color space because the complementary color pairs blue/yellow and red/green lie opposite each other (Figure 2.12.1).

By way of an actual example, CIELAB coordinates of L^* 74.8, a^* 50.1, b^* 49.4 specify a bright orange because of the relatively high L^* value and positive a^* and b^* values, which signify red and yellow color content.

Any L^*, a^*, b^* deviation would constitute a different color that may not visually match the bright orange described in the previous example, depending on the deviation's magnitude.

Software interfaced with spectrophotometers can calculate L^*, a^*, b^* coordinates and compare them to standards to show the absolute L^*, a^*, b^* values and ΔL^*, Δa^*, Δb^* or variation from a standard graphically. Typically, the standard's a^* and b^* coordinates are plotted at the intersection of

Figure 2.12.1.
CIELAB color space.

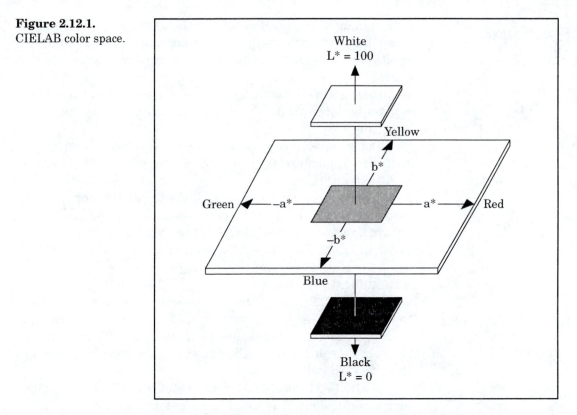

the a* and b* axes in the center of the color space, which is not its absolute position but a point of reference. Unless the sample has the exact same coordinate values, it will be displayed in one of the four quadrants showing the sample's deviation from the standard and the direction of the deviation. The L* value is usually shown along a vertical line with a scale alongside it, marked 0 at the bottom and 100 at the top. The standard's L* value is plotted at the 50 mark, again not to show the standard's absolute position but as a point of reference. The sample's deviation will again be shown as a function of its distance from the standard (Figure 2.12.2).

This type of color measurement system, by processing the relevant color stimuli and color dimensions using advanced measurement hardware, produces the most accurate and complete information of color that can be used for analytic interpretation and correction during the production phase of printed products.

The measure for print quality is essentially the degree to which a printed image is a facsimile of an original or OK sheets approved at various organizational levels. As such, the described CIELAB system is an excellent means to mea-

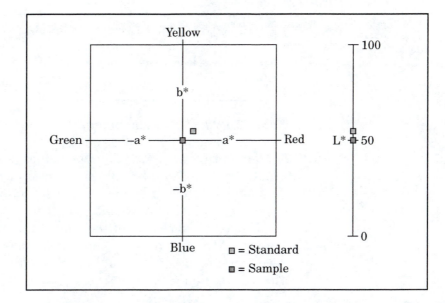

Figure 2.12.2.
A sample's deviation as a function of its distance from the standard.

sure the level of print quality and to set quality standards because the quality evaluation is based on objective numeric values.

Offsetting the advantages of the system somewhat is the high degree of complexity due to its reliance on three values. The ΔE^* simplifies the system by mathematically converting ΔL^*, Δa^*, Δb^* values into a single color difference value, but what is gained in reduced complexity is lost in analytical information.

At least one manufacturer uses ΔE^* values in the measuring unit that measures and controls press output and ink flow. The unit measures the deviation of a color bar's gray balance patches from a stored "perfect" gray and displays it as ΔL^*, Δa^*, b^*, and ΔE^* values. The visual significance of various ΔE values has been specified by this press manufacturer and is shown in Table 2.12.1.

The Canadian and U.S. Government Printing Offices also specify ΔE^* values for various quality levels, as shown in

Table 2.12.1.
Visual significance of ΔE^* values.

ΔE^*	Color Difference
up to 1	Very small
1 to 2	Small
2 to 3.5	Medium
3.5 to 5	Clear
over 5	Marked

Table 2.12.2.
Allowable ΔE*
deviations.

Quality Level	Allowable ΔE* Deviation
I	2.0
II	3.0
III	4.0

Table 2.12.2. It must be noted, however, that these ΔE* values are for solid spot colors only.

Calculating ΔL*, Δa*, and Δb* values is a matter of subtracting L*, a*, and b* values of a measured press sheet from the L*, a*, and b* values of a standard such as the measured values of a proof or OK sheet.

ΔE is the square root of the sum of the individually squared ΔL*, Δa*, and Δb* values. All information about the direction and magnitude of hue, chroma, and value is lost in this conversion.

ΔL*, Δa*, Δb*, and ΔE* Equations

$$\Delta L^* = L^*_{Sample} - L^*_{Standard}$$

$$\Delta a^* = a^*_{Sample} - a^*_{Standard}$$

$$\Delta b^* = b^*_{Sample} - b^*_{Standard}$$

$$\Delta E^* = \sqrt{\Delta L^{*2} + \Delta a^{*2} + \Delta b^{*2}}$$

where *sample* means the measured press sheet and *standard* means a proof, OK sheet, or a computer-stored value.

Example

If a bright orange spot color yields L* = 74.8, a* = 50.1, and b* = 49.4 values and the OK sheet that was approved by the customer has L* = 73.2, a* = 54.3, and b* = 51.5 values, the ΔL*, Δa*, Δb*, and ΔE* values are:

$$\Delta L^* = 74.8 - 73.2$$

$$= 1.6$$

$$\Delta a^* = 50.1 - 54.3$$

$$= -4.2$$

$$\Delta b^* = 49.4 - 51.5$$

$$= -2.1$$

$$\Delta E^* = \sqrt{1.6^2 + (-4.2)^2 + (-2.1)^2}$$

$$= \sqrt{2.56 + 17.64 + 4.41}$$

$$= \sqrt{24.61}$$

$$= 4.960846702$$

$$\approx 5.0$$

According to Table 2.12.1, a ΔE^* of 5.0 indicates a clear color difference.

13   Chroma and Hue Angle

The value and intensity of a color as well as a numeric designation of its hue can be expressed by a color notational system called CIELCH where L, C, and h indicate value, chroma, and hue, respectively. In the CIELAB and CIELUV spaces, color plots are located by the distance of a point relative to three planes. (For further information on CIELAB and CIELUV color spaces, refer to section 12.)

In the CIELCH color notational system chroma (C) is indicated by means of the distance or radius of a point from a fixed center. The angle made by a line that connects the center and the point indicates the hue angle (h). This color notational system is the result of a mathematical transformation from a Cartesian to a polar coordinate system and as such does not represent a distinct color space (Figure 2.13.1).

Chroma (C) and h are calculated from CIELAB a*, b* or CIELUV u*, v* values, while the L* value remains unconverted.

Figure 2.13.1.
CIELCH color
notation system.

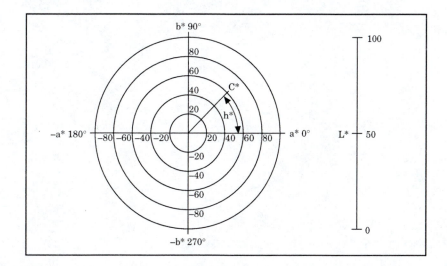

Chroma and Hue Angle Equations

$$\text{Chroma (C)} = \sqrt{a^{*2} + b^{*2}} \text{ or } \sqrt{u^{*2} + v^{*2}}$$

$$\text{Hue angle (h)} = \arctan\left(\frac{b^*}{a^*}\right) \text{ or } \arctan\left(\frac{v^*}{u^*}\right)$$

Example

If a bright orange spot color yields L* = 74.8, a* = 50.1, and b* = 49.4 values, then the converted CIELCH values are:

$$L = 74.8$$

$$\text{Chroma (C)} = \sqrt{50.1^2 + 49.4^2}$$

$$= \sqrt{2510.01 + 2440.36}$$

$$= \sqrt{4950.37}$$

$$= 70.35886582$$

$$\approx 70.4$$

$$\text{Hue angle (h)} = \arctan\left(\frac{49.4}{50.1}\right)$$

$$= \arctan 0.986027944$$

$$= 44.59692076$$

$$\approx 44.6$$

14 Ink Consumption

The cost of ink could be a substantial factor ranging from approximately 2 to 10% of the total cost for printed products. When planning a job, the approximate amount of ink required could be one of the more difficult cost estimation aspects. A number of relatively intangible factors such as the type and color of ink, the type and finish of paper used, the image-to-no-image ratio, the size of a job, and the run length have profound effects on ink consumption that are not easily defined.

Purchasing too much ink to complete a job carries with it unnecessary inventory costs and the added possibility of waste due to printing ink's limited shelf life.

Purchasing ink short of the amount required to complete a job is equally harmful to the printer because expensive printing machinery will be idled, resulting in costly downtime.

Ink estimation charts are available to assist printers in calculating reasonably accurate estimates for ink consumption. A computer program based on information available from ink estimation charts is one of the functions included with the software appended to this book.

It must be remembered that ink estimates obtained from charts and computer programs are at best good approximations. The constant factors used are the product of empirical data derived from tests and necessarily cannot be representative of the infinitely variable conditions possible.

However, some general recommendations for ink consumption apply in most instances and can be useful to the practicing estimator.

Paper requires varying amounts of ink because of the degree to which different types of paper absorb ink. (For more information on ink absorption, refer to section 9.) The papers in Table 2.14.1 are listed according to their relative ink consumption.

Table 2.14.1.
Ink consumption by type of paper, from least to most.

Enamel paper
Coated paper
Matte and dull coated paper
Uncoated paper

The color of ink necessitates varying amounts of ink by virtue of the coloring or tinctorial strength provided by the pigments used to produce different colors. The ink colors in Table 2.14.2 are listed according to the relative amounts of inks required on enamel papers.

Table 2.14.2.
Relative amounts of ink required, from least to most.

Black inks
Overprint varnishes and transparent bases
Green and purple inks
Magenta inks
Process yellow and cyan inks
Silver inks
Fluorescent inks
Metallic inks
Opaque white inks

Most ink-estimation charts consider text forms as a starting point, allowing for incremental ink consumption increases as the estimated ratio of solid image area to text image area changes toward greater solid image area content. For example, the computer program included with the software appended to this book uses a scale of one to ten to estimate image area content, allowing an increase of 1% ink consumption for each additional point on the scale.

The most tangible factors of ink consumption estimates are run length and image size. The amount of ink consumed changes in direct proportion to changes in these factors. This is to say, if image size or run length are decreased by 50%, ink consumption also decreases by 50%.

Ink Consumption Equation

Ink consumption =

$$\left(\frac{\text{Image area in inches} \times \text{Run length} \times \text{Image area type}}{\text{Ink and paper} \times 1{,}000} \right)$$

where *image area* is the image area in square inches, and *run length* is the number of sheets printed. *Image area type* is a constant factor that increases with greater solid image content. Text forms are assigned a value of 1.0 and completely solid forms have a value of 1.1. Any value between 1.0 and 1.1 is possible depending on the estimated amount of solid image area content. For example, a form with an estimated solid image area of 50% would be assigned a value of 1.05. *Ink and paper* is a constant factor that changes with the ink color and paper type used. The values assigned to different ink color and paper combinations are listed in Table 2.14.3.

Table 2.14.3.
Ink and paper
constant factors.

Paper Type	Enamel	Coated	Matte or Dull Coated	Uncoated
Black	425	390	375	275
Overprint varnish	400	375	350	
Tint base, transparent	400	380	375	250
Greens	360	350	335	235
Purples	360	350	335	235
Process yellow	355	355	340	225
Cyan	355	340	335	220
Magenta	350	345	340	225
Silver	335	300	285	220
Fluorescent	270	240	240	160
Metallic	215	200	200	130
Opaque white	200	175	165	135

Example 1

If a 17×21-in. image area for a brochure consists of an estimated 70% text and 30% solids, the approximate weight of black ink in pounds to print 175,000 sheets on coated paper is:

Ink consumption =

$$\left(\frac{17 \times 21 \times 175{,}000 \times 1.03}{390 \times 1{,}000}\right)$$

$$= \left(\frac{64{,}349{,}250}{390{,}000}\right)$$

$$= 164.9980769$$

$$\approx 165 \text{ lb.}$$

This result must be understood as an average value, which could deviate somewhat from actual amounts of ink consumed. If more accurate ink consumption estimates that reflect the actual production environment are required, an ink consumption test has to be performed. The test's results are then used to adjust the ink and paper constant.

How Can the Ink Consumption Method Be Improved to Reflect Actual Production Methods and Raw Materials?

Actual press test runs yield the most reliable results for ink consumption, especially when long runs are involved. A known weight of ink is placed in the ink fountain and, upon completion of the pressrun, the remaining ink is weighed. This remainder is subtracted from the original amount of ink. The result of this subtraction gives the actual amount of ink consumed in this particular production environment. To adjust the ink and paper constant factor, divide it by the actual amount of ink consumed and subtract the actual ink consumption from the calculated ink consumption. Now multiply the result of the subtraction by the result of the division, which gives the required adjustment value. If the actual ink consumption is larger than the calculated ink consumption, subtract the adjustment value from the ink and paper constant factor; otherwise, add the adjustment value to the ink and paper constant factor.

This adjusted ink and paper constant factor reflects the conditions and raw materials of the production environment that produced the printed sheets. Provided the production variables do not change, it will produce accurate ink consumption estimates with all subsequent pressruns.

Paper and Ink Constant Adjustment Procedure

$$A = \frac{\text{Ink and paper constant}}{\text{Actual amount of ink consumed}}$$

$$B = \text{Actual amount of ink consumed} - \text{Calculated amount of ink consumed}$$

$$\text{Adjustment} = A \times B$$

$$\text{New constant} = \text{Ink and paper constant} + \text{adjustment}$$
$$\textit{or} \quad \text{Ink and paper constant} - \text{adjustment}$$

If the adjustment value is positive, it is subtracted from the constant value; if it is negative, it is added to the constant value.

Example 2   If a pressrun having the exact same specification as described in example 1 results in a total ink consumption of 180 lb., then the adjusted ink and paper constant is:

$$A = \frac{390}{180}$$

$$= 2.166666667$$

$$B = 180 - 165$$

$$= 15$$

$$\text{Adjustment} = 2.166666667 \times 15 = 32.5$$

$$\text{New constant} = 390 - 32.5$$

$$= 357.5$$

Part 3
Type

The graphic communications industry stands alone among industries in its use of a unique unit of measurement called the point system. The point is a unit of length that is neither based on the metric nor on any other customary systems of measurement.

Anyone involved with graphic design must become familiar with the point system, as it is the unit of measurement for specifying typographical dimensions such as type sizes, line spacing, and column lengths.

In section 1, the point system and all of its derived units are discussed with regard to conversions between different units of measurements, the appropriate application of the point system, and recommended typesetting standards.

Section 2 deals with the nomenclature of type and the significance of point measures relative to the visible portions of type. The proportionality of type and mathematical methods to calculate the size of typographical elements are also discussed in this section.

Most people will be familiar with a standard unit of measurement from a personal reference point of view, such as a bed being approximately 2 m long or a standard ceiling having an approximate height of 8 ft. Similarly, it is a considerable advantage for someone working professionally with type to develop an ability to visualize type in terms of the point system. Visual examples included in both sections make a small contribution toward this end.

1 The Point System

Conventional linear measurement systems such as the metric and imperial systems do not lend themselves conveniently to the measurement of type fonts because the finely gradated type size ranges would result in unwieldy fractional values that are not easily remembered or calculated. Efforts to develop and standardize type measurement systems date back to the 1700s and are a testimonial to the technologically advanced conditions prevailing in the printing industry of that time.

The American point system has been in use for more than 100 years and, although type is now set electronically, continues to be the predominant system for specifying and measuring type sizes in most of the English-speaking world. Predating American attempts to standardize type size measurements were developments by French type founders Fournier and Didot. In 1887 the United States Typefounders Association adopted Fournier's system, first devised in 1737. Most European countries and the Americas, notably Brazil, use the Didot system. In recent years European type founders have introduced the metric system to specify type sizes, a development not widely adopted in North America.

The American point system's exact conversion factor is 1 point to 0.01383 in., which works out to exactly 72.3065799 points per inch, but to facilitate calculation it is often rounded to 72 points per inch without sacrificing accuracy substantially (Figure 3.1.1).

The Didot system has a conversion factor of 1 point to 0.01483 inches, or 67.43088334 points per inch, which renders this point unit slightly larger than the American point unit.

All further discussion will focus on the American point system because of its nearly complete adoption in the United

Figure 3.1.1.
Point, pica, agate, and
inch comparison
(enlarged 3×).

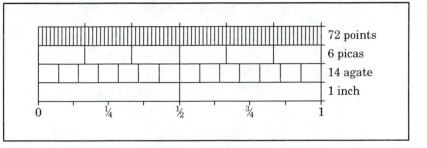

States, Canada, and the English-speaking world in general
and because of both systems' conceptual similarities.

Points are used primarily for specifying type sizes and
leading or the spacing between lines (Figures 3.1.2 and 3.1.3).

Figure 3.1.2.
Font sizes in points.

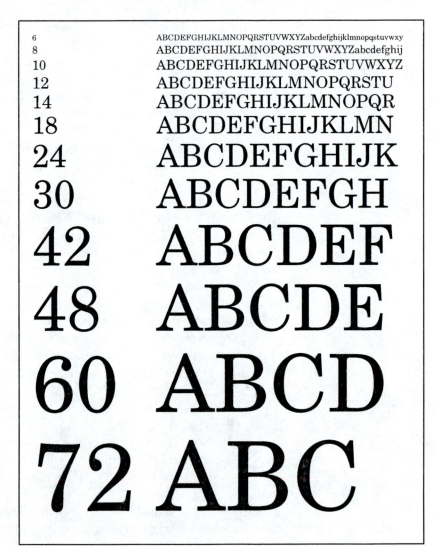

Figure 3.1.3.
Three paragraphs of 9-pt. type set with different amounts of leading.

Conventional linear measurement systems such as the metric and imperial systems do not lend themselves conveniently to the measurement of type fonts because the finely gradated type size ranges would result in unwieldy fractional values that are not easily remembered or calculated. Efforts to develop and standardize type measurement systems date back to the 1700s and are a testimonial to the technologically advanced conditions prevailing in the printing industry of that time.

The previous paragraph was set with 20% default leading, or a 10.8-pt. baseline-to-baseline distance.

Conventional linear measurement systems such as the metric and imperial systems do not lend themselves conveniently to the measurement of type fonts because the finely gradated type size ranges would result in unwieldy fractional values that are not easily remembered or calculated. Efforts to develop and standardize type measurement systems date back to the 1700s and are a testimonial to the technologically advanced conditions prevailing in the printing industry of that time.

The previous paragraph was set with 7-pt. leading, or a 16-pt. baseline-to-baseline distance.

Conventional linear measurement systems such as the metric and imperial systems do not lend themselves conveniently to the measurement of type fonts because the finely gradated type size ranges would result in unwieldy fractional values that are not easily remembered or calculated. Efforts to develop and standardize type measurement systems date back to the 1700s and are a testimonial to the technologically advanced conditions prevailing in the printing industry of that time.

The previous paragraph was set with 12-pt. leading, or a 21-pt. baseline-to-baseline distance.

The amount of spacing between lines depends on the type style and size used. Most desktop publishing software allows by default for 20% of type size. For instance, the three text blocks in Figure 3.1.3 were set in a 9-pt. font. The upper block has the 20% default leading, which means 9 pt. + 1.8 pt., or 10.8-pt. baseline-to-baseline distance. The middle block has 7-pt. leading, or 16-pt. baseline-to-baseline distance. The bottom block has 12-pt. leading, or 21-pt. baseline-to-baseline distance. Table 3.1.1 shows the recommended text leading for a number of type sizes.

Table 3.1.1.
Recommended text leading.

Type size	Minimum leading	Maximum leading
6 points	Solid	1 point
8 points	Solid	2 points
10 points	Solid to 2 points	4 points
11 points	1 point	4 points
12 points	2 points	6 points
14 points	3 points	8 points

The pica unit is used whenever larger dimensions have to be quantified. It measures exactly 12 pt. and is the unit of measurement for line lengths, the vertical dimension or depth of text, and other image areas (Figure 3.1.1).

Not unlike leading, the length of lines is also governed by type size. The larger the type size is, the longer a line should be. All the same, a typesetter should be guided by the general principle that very long or very short lines are difficult to read. Table 3.1.2 shows the recommended column length ranges for a variety of type sizes. A rule of thumb for good book legibility is seven to ten words per line.

While the column widths listed in Table 3.1.2 are usually flexible enough to accommodate different type fonts, another

Table 3.1.2.
Recommended column widths.

Type size	Minimum width	Maximum width
6 points	8 picas	10 picas
8 points	9 picas	13 picas
10 points	13 picas	16 picas
11 points	13 picas	18 picas
12 points	14 picas	21 picas
14 points	18 picas	24 picas
18 points	24 picas	30 picas

Figure 3.1.4.
Basing column widths
on one and one-half
lowercase alphabet
lengths.

abcdefghijklmnopqrstuvwxyzabcdefghijklm
Very wide or narrow columns are hard to
read. Column width depends on the point
size and the typeface being used. Small
typeface require narrow columns, because
the eye tends to focus on a narrower range.
Columns set too wide could cause the
reader to miss the beginning of each successive line. Columns set too narrow
require undue back and forth scanning by
the eye, causing discomfort and fatigue for
prolonged reading.

6-pt. Bookman

abcdefghijklmnopqrstuvwxyzabcdefghijklm
Very wide or narrow columns are hard to
read. Column width depends on the point
size and the typeface being used. Small
typeface require narrow columns, because
the eye tends to focus on a narrower range.
Columns set too wide could cause the
reader to miss the beginning of each successive line. Columns set too narrow require
undue back and forth scanning by the eye,
causing discomfort and fatigue for prolonged reading.

10-pt. Goudy

abcdefghijklmnopqrstuvwxyzabcdefghijklm
Very wide or narrow columns are hard to
read. Column width depends on the point
size and the typeface being used. Small typeface require narrow columns, because the
eye tends to focus on a narrower range.
Columns set too wide could cause the
reader to miss the beginning of each successive line. Columns set too narrow require
undue back and forth scanning by the eye,
causing discomfort and fatigue for prolonged reading.

14-pt. Century Old Style

method postulates that column widths should be equal to one and one-half lowercase alphabet lengths, in the style and size that the column is set. This method, shown in Figure 3.1.4, agrees reasonably well with the column width values in Table 3.1.2.

Type size is to a large degree a function of end-use requirement. It would make little sense to use large 18-pt. type for voluminous reference texts, as this would result in an unreasonably large number of pages or book volumes. Likewise, a first-grade reader set in 6-pt. type would challenge a young and beginning reader unnecessarily. Table 3.1.3 lists a number of type sizes and their end-use application.

Table 3.1.3. Recommended type sizes.

Type Size	Application
6, 7, 8, 9 points	Reference books, lexicons, catalogs, the fine print in contracts
10, 11, 12 points	Books, magazines, any printed piece that requires sustained reading
16, 18, 24 points	Small headings
36, 48, 72 points	Elements that must stand out, such as title pages or chapter titles

The term *agate lines* signifies the vertical distance of newspaper columns and is to this day a popular if not a predominant measure of quantifying and pricing advertising lineage in newspapers. An agate line is exactly one-fourteenth of an inch (Figure 3.1.1). This unit of measurement has its roots in the tendency of late 19th and early 20th century newspapers to use extremely small 5.5-pt. agate type for its advertisement columns, a practice that resulted in 14 such lines taking up one inch. Today, many classified ads are still quite small but usually do not result in quite as much crowding as the newspapers of old, yet the agate unit of measurement is still in use.

Calculating the cost of advertisements is a matter of determining the number of agate lines contained in an ad, multiplied by the rate charged per agate line. For instance, if the cost per agate line is $3, then a four-column ad that is 3.5 in. deep would cost $588 ($3.5 \times 14 = 49$ agate lines per column, 49×4 columns = 196 agate lines, and 196 agate lines $\times$ $3 per agate line = $588).

U.S. Points to Inches Equation

Inches = U.S. points × 0.01383

Example: A 144-pt. (U.S.) display type is how many inches high?

Inches = 144 × 0.01383

= 1.99152

Inches to U.S. Points Equation

U.S. points = Inches × 72.30658

For ease of calculation a conversion factor of 72 pt. to the inch is often used without affecting the accuracy substantially.

Example: The width of a 1.5625-in.-wide capital "W" letter is how many U.S. points wide?

U.S. points = 1.5625 × 72.30658

= 112.9790313

≈ 113 pt.

U.S. Points to Millimeters Equation

Millimeters = U.S. points × 0.351

Example: A 144-pt. (U.S.) display type measures how many millimeters?

Millimeters = 144 × 0.351

= 50.544 millimeters

Millimeters to U.S. Points Equation

U. S. Points = Millimeters × 2.8467157

Example: The width of a 40-mm-wide capital letter "W" measures how many U.S. points?

U.S. points = 40 × 2.8467157

= 113.868628

≈ 114 pt.

**U.S. Points to
Picas Equation**

$$\text{Picas} = \text{Points} \div 12$$
$$\text{Remainder points} = \text{Points} - (\text{Picas} \times 12)$$

Example: A 242-pt.-wide space allowed for a column measures how many picas and remaining points?

$$\text{Picas} = 242 \div 12$$

$$= 20.16666666$$

$$\approx 20 \text{ picas}$$

$$\text{Remainder points} = 242 - (20 \times 12)$$

$$= 2 \text{ points}$$

**Picas to
U.S. Points
Equation**

$$\text{Points} = \text{Picas} \times 12$$

Example: How many points are there in an 18-picas-long line?

$$\text{Points} = 18 \times 12$$

$$= 216 \text{ pt.}$$

**Inches to
Agate Lines
Equation**

$$\text{Agate lines} = \text{Inches} \times 14$$

Example: If a daily newspaper charges \$2.75 per agate line, how much will a two-column-wide classified ad that is 2.25 in. deep cost?

$$\text{Agate lines} = 2.25 \times 14 \times 2 = 63$$

$$\text{Cost of ad} = 63 \times \$2.75$$

$$= \$173.25$$

**Agate Lines to
Inches Equation**

$$\text{Inches} = \text{Agate lines} \div 14$$

Example: The depth of a one-column-wide ad in inches that has 49 agate lines is:

$$\text{Inches} = 49 \div 14 = 3.5$$

Inches to Didot Points Equation

$$\text{Didot points} = \text{Inches} \times 67.43088334$$

Example: The width of a 1.25-in.-wide capital letter "W" in Didot points is:

$$\text{Didot points} = 1.25 \times 67.43088334$$

$$= 84.28860418$$

$$\approx 84.29$$

Millimeters to Didot Points Equation

$$\text{Didot points} = \text{Millimeters} \times 2.6548$$

Example: The width of a 40-mm-wide capital letter "W" in Didot points is:

$$\text{Didot points} = 40 \times 2.6548$$

$$= 106.192$$

$$\approx 106 \text{ Didot points}$$

Didot Points to Millimeters Equation

$$\text{Millimeters} = \text{Didot points} \times 0.3759$$

Example: A 144-Didot-pt. display type is how many millimeters?

$$\text{Millimeters} = 144 \times 0.3759 = 54.1296$$

$$\approx 54 \text{ Didot points}$$

Didot Points to Inches Equation

$$\text{Inches} = \text{Didot points} \times 0.0148$$

Example: A 144-Didot-pt. display type is how many inches?

$$\text{Inches} = 144 \times 0.0148 = 2.1312$$

Didot Points to U.S. Points Equation

$$\text{U.S. points} = \text{Didot points} \times 1.07$$

Example: A European 24-Didot-pt. type font is how many U.S. points?

$$\text{U.S. points} = 24 \times 1.07 = 25.68$$

**U.S. Points
to Didot Points
Equation**

Didot points = U.S. points × 0.93256

Example: A 24-pt. (U.S.) font measures how many Didot points?

U.S. points = 24 × 0.93256 = 22.381

2   The x-Height of Letters

Type design dates back many centuries, evoking memories of venerable type designers like William Caslon or William Morris. Their type designs were created at a time when printing text was the domain of relief printing processes, which required the casting of an individual piece of metal, having on its surface the relief of a character. This process resulted in pieces of metal type or "type," a term that continues to be used in the modern-day graphic communications industry with terminology such as typeface, type style, type font, typesetting, typography, or simply type.

A rudimentary knowledge of this now-obsolete typesetting method is helpful, however, in understanding typesetting in the electronic age. Computer-based text-generation systems are in part based on metal type technology, not only in terms of nomenclature but also with regard to technical constraints of typeface design and type sizes. Figure 3.2.1 shows a piece of foundry type of a 24-pt. capital letter "P." Notice that the 24-pt. dimension indicates the dimensions across the edges of the type piece, or body of type, as typesetters used to call it. The letter itself is somewhat shorter than the body; in fact, the exact dimensions of the letter are not known. The need for line spacing is the most obvious reason why letters are shorter than the type body, as otherwise the letters

Figure 3.2.1.
Foundry type.

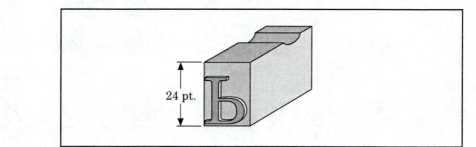

would touch each other when set in multiple lines. The other less obvious reason is related to the type designer's aesthetic sensibility. Type designers will strive for perfect harmony in their letter creations, of which the letter proportions are an important component. The analogy of a painter's canvas to the space available on a piece of type is quite appropriate because in both cases the artists use the available space to achieve visually satisfying results. If there is one difference between the canvas of old and the canvas today, it is that the boundaries of the former canvas embodied by the physical piece of type were visible, while today's digital type, which still requires these boundaries, is invisible.

Type sizes are specified using the point system, and we still refer to a font's point size as its body size. Upon closer examination, the actual size of text characters is not accurately conveyed by the nominal type size of a font, but can at best provide only an approximation of font size. Figure 3.2.2 shows ten lowercase pairs of "d" and "g" characters of different typefaces having identical 28-pt. type sizes. The distance between the fullest ascending d's and the fullest descending g's is indicated by two lines, 28 pt. apart from each other. None of the typefaces touch both lines and several have spaces to varying degrees, which means none of the typefaces are actually 28 pt. high and some are substantially smaller than 28 pt. Typefaces 8 and 9 demonstrate this lack of absolute correlation between the nominal and actual sizes of typefaces. Typeface 8 extends almost to the ascender and descender lines, while typeface 9 has considerable space between both lines.

A third line, called the baseline, indicates the position on which all letters, including capital letters, rest. As shown in Figure 3.2.2, the relative extension of descenders and ascenders from the baseline varies greatly from font to font. This

Figure 3.2.2.
Ten type fonts of lowercase 28-pt. letters.

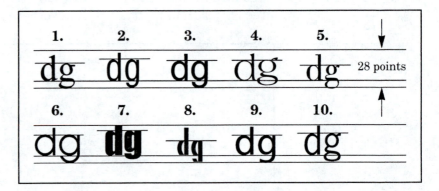

variation is particularly pronounced when comparing ascenders of type fonts 7 and 8, and when comparing descenders of type fonts 4 and 5.

One last dimensional variation that distinguishes type fonts is the so-called x-height of letters. The x-height signifies the height of the majority of lowercase letters—such as a, c, e, i, m...x—that have neither ascenders nor descenders. The term x-height is used because the lowercase "x" is the only lowercase letter whose four terminals touch the baseline and upper limit of lowercase letters symmetrically (Figure 3.2.3).

Figure 3.2.3.
Main type proportions of 60-pt. Helvetica Condensed.

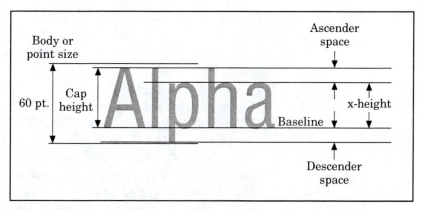

The x-height, maybe more than any other letter dimension, characterizes a type style because of its dominant visual effect and influence on the actual and perceived dimensions of ascenders in particular. Exemplifying typefaces with very large and very small x-heights are typefaces 7 and 8, respectively (Figure 3.2.2). Notice how the extremely large x-height of typeface 7 tends to shorten the ascender, giving the typeface a larger point size appearance than its size. The exact opposite effect can be observed in typeface 8, which has an extremely small x-height.

Aside from aesthetic preferences, the legibility of typefaces must be taken into consideration. Toward this end, typefaces with small x-heights usually require more leading than typefaces with large x-heights.

The overriding theme of this discussion can be summarized in stating that type sizes are standardized only to the extent that they can have a wide range of sizes that can never be larger in height than their nominal point size.

Attempts to standardize type sizes have been made, notably in Germany, where many of the newer typefaces

have standard capital letter heights. The trend to standardize type sizes is driven by a desire to increase production
efficiency and to overcome problems of digital font compati-
bility, which has the unfortunate consequence of limiting
artistic expression and typeface diversity.

There is, however, one type size-related factor that is constant, the proportion of all typeface elements relative to each
other. No matter how large or how small a type font is, the
relative dimensions of x-height, ascenders, and descenders
will always remain the same and can therefore be calculated
and predicted.

If, for example, a 60-pt. typeface has a measured x-height
of 30 pt., then the ratio of point size to x-height is $^{60}\!/_{30}$ or 2. It
follows that a 28-pt. typeface will have an x-height of $^{28}\!/_{2}$ or
14 pt. Similarly, the cap height, ascender to descender
height, and lowercase letters (or, for that matter, any letter's
real size) could be calculated.

Once the ratio of the point size to measured type element
is known, it can be put to use for the exact opposite purpose
of determining the point size necessary to fill a space measuring a given dimension. For instance, the point size
required to fill a vertical space measuring 88 pt. with a font
having a cap height of 44 pt. at a point size of 60 pt. would be
calculated by first determining the point size to cap height
ratio $^{60}\!/_{44}$, or 1.3636, followed by multiplying this ratio by the
space available, 88 × 1.3636, or 120 pt.

The accuracy of this method depends on the precision of
the measured dimension, which is more easily achieved
when measuring extremely large point sizes such as 60- or
72-pt. typefaces. A practical, but not unimportant, matter is
the type of measuring instrument used. Transparent rulers
or line gauges with point gradations are most suitable for
this method because they could be laid over and aligned with
the type elements to be measured.

One example for practical application of this method is the
design stage of extremely large display type, including outdoor signs, murals, and billboards, in order to calculate space
requirements or point sizes to fill given spaces.

True Type Dimension Equation

$$Factor = \frac{Point\ size\ of\ type}{Measured\ type\ dimension}$$

$$True\ type\ dimension = \frac{New\ point\ size}{Factor}$$

where *measured type dimension* is ascender-to-descender height, cap height, letter width, or any other measured type element. *Point size of type* is the nominal point size of the type. *New point size* is the nominal point size of type for which the true dimension is not known.

Example 1

If the ascender-to-descender dimension of a 60-pt. Helvetica Condensed typeface measures 56 pt., then the ascender-to-descender distance of a 28-pt. typeface of the same font is:

$$\text{Factor} = \frac{60}{56}$$

$$= 1.071428571$$

$$\text{True type dimension} = \frac{28}{1.071428571}$$

$$= 26.13333334 \text{ pt.}$$

This result for example 1 can be verified by measuring the measured type dimensions in Figures 3.2.3 and 3.2.2, typeface 2.

Example 2

The word Alpha, below, is set in 28-pt. Helvetica Condensed typeface.

Alpha

If the measured length of this word set in 60-pt. type is 131 pt., the width of the above word set in 28 pt. will be:

$$\text{Factor} = \frac{60}{131}$$

$$= 0.4580152$$

$$\text{True type dimension} = \frac{28}{0.4580152}$$

$$= 61.1 \text{ pt.}$$

The result for example 2 can be verified by measuring the word widths in Figure 3.2.3 and in the example itself.

Point Size Required to Fill Available Space Equation

$$Factor = \frac{Point\ size\ of\ type}{Measured\ type\ dimension}$$

Point size = Available space × Factor

Example

The word NORMAN, below, is set in 48-pt. Helvetica Condensed Light.

NORMAN

If the measured length of the word is 156 pt. long; the point size necessary to fill a 189-pt. space will be:

$$Factor = \frac{48}{156}$$

$$= 0.307692307$$

$$Point\ size = 189 \times 0.307692307$$

$$= 58.15384602$$

$$\approx 58\ pt.$$

Part 4
Prepress

Within the past 15 years, the prepress area has transformed from a largely photomechanical to an electronic imaging process. Yet the basic function of prepress operations remains more or less what it has always been, namely, the generation of images and the preparation of image carriers for the purpose of reproduction in a printing process. The implementation of this new technology for the same ultimate purpose means that many new technological concepts have to be learned, while a number of old concepts are still relevant and must be retained.

Electronic imaging, unlike now-obsolete photomechanical methods, is dependent to a large degree on the digital electronic computer. An understanding of fundamental computer principles therefore becomes an essential requirement to exploit the tremendous image-processing potential of computers, as well as to discern the inherent limitations of digital, visual information processed by computers.

The sections in this part of the book deal with the computation of gray levels, file sizes, scanning resolutions, output resolutions, gradient fill steps, radius values for unsharp masking, scaling, and scanning resolution for multimedia.

Some topics, such as file-size computations, are completely new concepts that had no relevancy in the pre-digital age. Others, such as unsharp masking, are mere digital reincarnations of old photomechanical techniques. Still others, such as scaling calculations, remain virtually unchanged from the bygone photomechanical era.

A category of topics that is relatively new for the graphic communications industry is best exemplified by section 4 on scanning resolution for video/multimedia. Many printers realize that they are well positioned to make forays into nonprint media markets because their already advanced electronic imaging infrastructure enables them to repurpose digital information relatively easily.

1 Gray Levels

The reproduction of multiple tones or gray levels is possible
only because of a technological sleight of hand that cheats
the eye into perceiving very small and closely spaced dots as
tonal variations. Medieval visual artists pioneered tonal
representation with techniques such as cross-hatching or
pointillism in drawings and engravings, which later evolved
into a mechanical method of tonal reproduction called
halftoning. Until about the 1970s, halftones were produced
using a so-called contact screen, which is a transparent film
of vignetted dots laid over light-sensitive film, producing dots
of infinitely varying sizes, depending on the intensity of light
reflected from the original.

The general principle of halftoning still applies today, but
the methods of production have changed from the analog
contact screen to digital methods. In digital halftone production, the halftone dot is made up of an even smaller image
element called a dot, spot, or pixel. (All further discussion
will refer to this image element as spot so as not to confuse it
with the halftone dot.) These spots range in size from a
coarse 64 spots per inch for dot matrix printers to extremely
fine 2,540 spots per inch (dpi) for imagesetters and platesetters.

The term digital implies that, in digital electronic computers, the binary 1s and 0s represent image and nonimage
areas, respectively. The binary number 1 represents the spot
or spots that make up a digital halftone dot within a defined
square area called a halftone cell; therefore, it is unlike its
infinitely variable analog counterpart, changing its size
according to a discrete number of units (Figure 4.1.1).

Because individual spots are too small for the eye to see,
varying numbers of spots per halftone cell are perceived as
tonal variations or gray levels (Figure 4.1.2).

Figure 4.1.1.
Binary halftone cell.

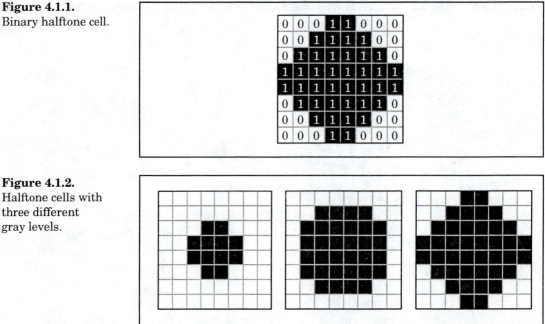

Figure 4.1.2.
Halftone cells with
three different
gray levels.

Even though the term used is gray level, it is not limited to tonal variation of black, but instead applies equally to any color, in which case tonal variation is perceived as varying shades of cyan, magenta, or yellow, for instance. Because each halftone matrix shown in Figure 4.1.2 is capable of producing 64 shades of one color, it has the theoretical potential to combine with the 64 shades of one or several other colors. This means that the number of possible colors that can be created with cyan, magenta, and yellow are calculated by multiplying the 64 shades possible for each color with each other; thus, $64 \times 64 \times 64 = 262{,}144$ colors.

Each digital halftone is assigned a halftone cell, the size of which is adjustable depending on the desired halftone screen frequency (Figure 4.1.3). The higher the halftone screen frequency, the more image information that can be described, resulting in a better image resolution or more truthful reproduction. The number of halftone cells fitting a linear inch is called the halftone screen ruling and can be 65 or 85 lines per inch (lpi) for newspapers, and 110, 120, 133, 150, and 200 lpi and higher for commercial printing.

The maximum number of gray levels depends on the output device resolution and the halftone screen ruling. The main output devices used in printing are imagesetters and, increasingly, platesetters for computer-to-plate imaging sys-

Figure 4.1.3.
Gray levels.

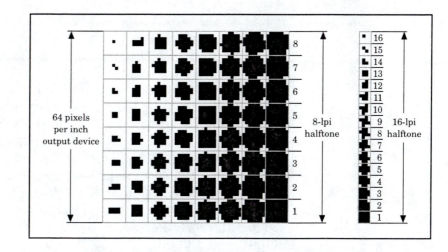

tems. Although many imagesetters and platesetters allow for incremental spot size selection of 635, 1,270, or 2,540 dpi, and some drum imagesetters have infinitely variable spot size adjustments, the spots per inch must be considered fixed to the extent that spot sizes do not change within a reproduction.

Because of the fixed number of output device spots per linear inch available to accommodate a given halftone screen ruling, higher screen rulings must necessarily have a smaller cell size than lower screen rulings. Consequently, higher or finer screen rulings, by virtue of their smaller cell areas and reduced number of spots per cell, produce fewer gray levels than lower and coarser screen rulings.

This principle is demonstrated in Figure 4.1.3*, where two halftone screen rulings of 8 and 16 lpi are shown together with their resulting gray levels produced on an output device having 64 spots per inch. Notice that doubling of halftone screen ruling results in quartering of the cell area, a ratio that is exactly reflected in the number of gray levels.

It can be seen that the mutual relationship of image resolution and the number of gray levels is a trade-off, wherein the increase of one decreases the other. The only possible option to achieve both high image resolution and a maximum number of gray levels is to reduce the output device's spot size. This option could be as simple as choosing an output device's smaller spot size level or as complicated and expensive as acquiring an output device capable of generating spot sizes small enough to achieve the desired number of gray levels.

---

*In order to make graphic representation of screen rulings and output resolutions possible, Figure 4.1.3 shows extremely large, nonstandard units.

The importance of high-resolution capability in output devices is demonstrated by the following example.

PostScript, a page description language widely used in the printing industry, supports 256 gray levels. Assuming that 256 gray levels are required and 133 lpi is the minimum halftone screen ruling to achieve an acceptable quality, the output resolution must be 2,540 dpi. This is because 256 gray levels require 16 spots in both the horizontal and vertical directions of each halftone cell, which, multiplied by 133, amounts to 2,128 spots per linear inch (16×133). Imagesetters with incremental steps of 1,270 and 2,540 dpi would therefore require the 2,540-dpi resolution to achieve both the 256 gray levels of PostScript and a modest halftone frequency of 133 lpi.

Number of Gray Levels Equation

$$\text{Number of gray levels} = \left(\frac{\text{Output resolution}}{\text{Halftone screen ruling}}\right)^2$$

Example 1

The number of gray levels that can be obtained from an imagesetter adjusted to an output resolution of 1,270 dpi, if the reproduction has a halftone screen ruling of 150 lpi, is:

$$\text{Number of gray levels} = \left(\frac{1,270}{150}\right)^2$$

$$= (8.466666666)^2$$

$$= 71.6844$$

$$\approx 72$$

Example 2

The number of gray levels that can be obtained from an imagesetter adjusted to an output resolution of 1,270 dpi, if the reproduction has a halftone screen ruling of 133 lpi, is:

$$\text{Number of gray levels} = \left(\frac{1,270}{133}\right)^2$$

$$= (9.54887218)^2$$

$$= 91.118$$

$$\approx 91$$

2 Scanning Resolution for Halftones

Capturing graphic images to be reproduced in any of the various printing processes requires a peripheral input device called a scanner. The three types of scanners are handheld, flatbed, and drum scanners. Handheld scanners are non-professional devices used mostly by hobbyists, while flatbed and drum scanners are used in the graphic communications industry. All scanners serve to digitize graphic images, storing them as digital data in a computer file, and can, if needed, be merged with text in word processing and page layout programs.

The quality and usefulness of scanners for professional application is in part rated by their ability to record the smallest details that a graphic image may hold. This is called the scanner's optical resolution and can range in flatbed scanners from 300 to 5,280 samples* per inch (spi) and in drum scanners from 2,000 to 24,000 spi. In practice, this means that image details smaller than 0.0033 in. (1 ÷ 300) are beyond the ability of a 300-spi scanner to be distinguished as separate entities, which is one reason why low-resolution scanners are not suitable for demanding quality reproductions. Additional demands on image resolution are effected by image enlargement.

Depending on the scanner model, scanning resolutions are adjusted at several levels, or they are infinitely variable on the basis of two parameters, enlargement factor and halftone screen ruling.

---

*Some texts and major software packages use the term pixel instead of sample; this text differentiates between pixels and samples, wherein a sample is a latent sensing or input unit and a pixel is the smallest possible output unit that a digital device can display.

The relationship of enlargement to resolution is linear, as every additional enlargement relative to the original requires an equal and proportional increase of scanned samples. Effectively, this means that, if an original's size is enlarged by 200%, the required scanning resolution doubles. Therefore, enlarging very small originals such as slides and transparencies without sacrificing image quality challenges the optical resolution resources of scanners, especially if great magnifications are needed. Some high-end drum scanners can produce enlargements of up to 3,000%, a feature that is beyond the capability of mid-range scanners because of their limited optical resolution.

Scans of original photographs or art with tonal variation that are destined for reproduction in any of the printing processes require the original's continuous tonal gradations to be converted into discontinuous dots of varying sizes. This process, called halftone, is described more fully in section 1.

Provided a scan is made the same size as the original, a scanning resolution equal to the halftone screen frequency should theoretically be sufficient because every scanned sample has enough information to build a halftone cell. However, this would only be true if both the sample and halftone dot orientations were identical. In reality, rows and columns of samples are aligned perfectly parallel to the vertical and horizontal planes, while rows and columns of halftone dots, depending on the color they represent, are aligned at various angles to the horizontal and vertical planes (with the exception of yellow). Different halftone screen angles for each process color are necessary to prevent moiré patterns, which are visually objectionable "swirl"-type patterns caused by lightwave interference when the halftone screen alignments for each of the four process colors are not correctly varied, as shown in Figure 4.2.1.

To compensate for the discrepancy of samples and halftone dot orientations, a so-called halftone factor is used when calculating scanning resolutions. There is no industry-wide agreement as to what the exact halftone factor should be, and, consequently, values ranging from 1.25 to 2.00 are used based on a practitioner's intuition and experience or blind acceptance of arbitrary values.

Notwithstanding this ambiguity, the rationale for halftone factors is based on mathematically definable parameters that, if applied, result in a rational starting point for standardizing scanning resolutions.

Figure 4.2.1.
Halftone screen
angles.*

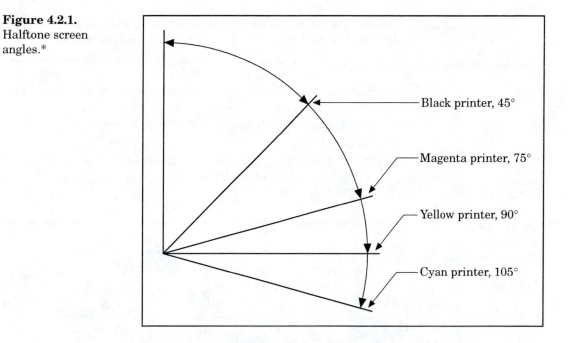

Black printer, 45°

Magenta printer, 75°

Yellow printer, 90°

Cyan printer, 105°

A sample-to-halftone dot ratio higher than 1:1 is needed because the scanning direction distance covered by a given number of samples is longer than the distance covered by the same number of halftone cells in the same direction (Figure 4.2.2). This results from the scanning direction being parallel to the vertical plane, while halftone screen angles are oblique.

Figure 4.2.2.
Scanning when sam-
ples per inch (spi) and
lines per inch (lpi) are
equal.

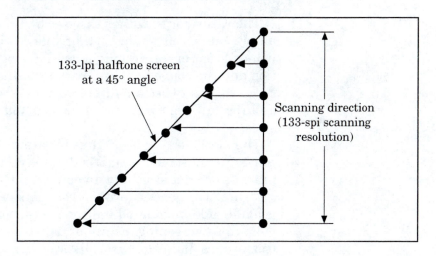

133-lpi halftone screen
at a 45° angle

Scanning direction
(133-spi scanning
resolution)

*Some screen angles such as 105° are not achievable in digital halftones because there is no integer value that results in this angle. So-called irrational tangent screening and supercells address this problem, yielding angles very close to those shown in Figure 4.2.1.

The spatial relationship of distances in the scanning, CCD array, and halftone dot directions is the same as the hypotenuse, and the lines form a right angle in a right angle triangle. It is thus possible to calculate the ratio by which the distance in one direction is foreshortened relative to the distance in the other direction because we know that the square on the hypotenuse is equal to the sum of the squares on the two other sides ($A^2 + B^2 = C^2$). The ratio of halftone screen frequency to samples for the black printer, with a screen angle of 45°, should therefore be A to $\sqrt{C^2}$, or 1:1.41 (Figure 4.2.3).

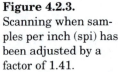

Figure 4.2.3.
Scanning when samples per inch (spi) has been adjusted by a factor of 1.41.

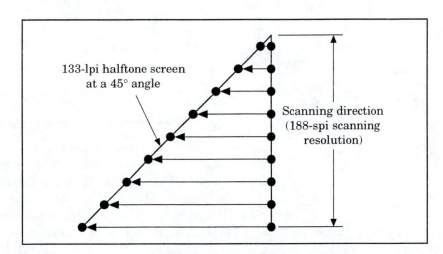

133-lpi halftone screen at a 45° angle

Scanning direction (188-spi scanning resolution)

The ratios for the other three colors would actually be even lower—in fact, it would be 1 for yellow—by reason of their non-existent or lesser obliqueness. Erring on the side of caution and the convenience of working with round numbers are good reasons to use a halftone factor of 2.0, which virtually assures sufficient image information and economical file sizes.

The methods discussed thus far are recommended for the conventional screening method based on the concept of varying halftone dot sizes and an equal number of dots per linear measure. The generic term for conventional halftone screening is amplitude-modulated halftone, as opposed to a newer type of halftone screening technique called frequency modulated (sometimes also called stochastic screening). In frequency-modulated halftones, the size of the dots remains constant, and tonal variation is achieved by varying the density or frequency of dots per unit area. One of the advantages of this halftone technique is the total absence of moiré patterns because screen angles are not required in stochastic screening. With no screen angles for which to be compensated, the halftone factor for scanning resolution could be as low as 1 and is seldom more than 1.2.

Regardless of calculated scanning resolutions, the best scanning results are achieved at the real size of the original and with scanning resolutions that are divisible into the maximum optical resolution of the scanner. This means that scanning resolutions for a 3,000 spi scanner should ideally be 1,500, 1,000, 750, 600, 500, 375, 300, 250, 200, 150, 125, 120, 100, and 75. Other scanning resolutions, while possible, will have the effect of diminishing the reproduction's fidelity because noninteger remainders lead to somewhat inaccurate averaging of sample values.

Most midrange to high-end scanners are quite capable of exceeding calculated scanning resolutions, which begs the question: Why isn't the maximum possible scanning resolution used for all scans?

There are two parts to the answer, the first of which is that higher-than-necessary scanning resolutions do not result in better quality. This is related to the way raster image processors (RIPs) process excessive samples. A RIP is a hardware device or software utility that electronically screens entire pages, generating so-called bitmaps for each color to be printed. Since the RIP has no way of distinguishing which samples are necessary and which are superfluous, it averages the sample values and distributes them to adjacent halftone cells. This could have the effect of simultaneously lightening some and darkening other adjacent halftone cells with the unfortunate consequence of reducing contrast and image definition.

The second part relates to the way scanning resolution affects workflow. Scanning resolution and the file size of an image are inextricably related. File sizes increase geometrically, or quadruple for every doubling of scanning resolution. For example, an 8×10-in. original scanned at a resolution of 200 spi in the CMYK mode would produce a file size of approximately 12,500 kilobytes (KB). The same image scanned at 400 spi would increase the file size to 50,000 KB. (For further information on file sizes, refer to section 6.) Larger file sizes are more costly to process for a variety of reasons, not the least of which is processing time. Larger-than-necessary file sizes slow down processing time on imagesetters or platesetters, the economic use of which can only be maximized with a speedy throughput and high volume of scans. Fast processing time is even more critical on computer-to-press systems because the productive capacity of a multimillion dollar press would be compromised.

Electronic file transfer to remote sites is slowed by larger-than-necessary files, resulting in increased telecommunication cost.

The amount of additional data arising from excessive file sizes may require more costly primary working memory or RAM and additional or more expensive data storage media. These are some of the compelling reasons for scanning only at resolutions needed to capture the information to reproduce graphic images truthfully and not beyond.

Scanning Resolution for Halftones Equation

Scanning resolution =

Halftone screen ruling × Halftone factor × Scale factor

Example

The scanning resolution for an original enlarged by 300%, printed with a halftone screen ruling of 133 lpi, is:

$$\text{Scanning resolution} = 133 \times 2 \times 300\%$$

$$= 266 \times 3$$

$$\approx 798 \text{ samples per inch}$$

3 Scanning Resolution for Continuous-Tone Printers

Continuous-tone printers, although producing images of deceivingly similar quality to continuous-tone originals, is a bit of a misnomer because tonal variation is created by discontinuous dots. The reason for this near continuous-tone quality is related to the capacity of some inkjet, dye sublimation, and thermal wax printers to print spots at more than one and sometimes at a great many levels of densities. In actuality, the amount of ink, dye, or wax transferred to the substrate varies, not unlike the varying amount of paint transferred by an artist's lighter or heavier brush stroke. This, however, occurs at the discrete level of printed spots and therefore cannot be considered a true continuous-tone reproduction.

The method for calculating scanning resolutions is nearly identical to the method used for halftones. (For further information on scanning resolutions for halftones, refer to section 2.) Since there are no halftone dots in images printed on continuous-tone printers, halftone angle compensation (halftone factor) is not required when calculating scanning resolutions for output on continuous-tone printers.

Output resolutions of some continuous-tone printing devices are often sufficiently high to warrant scanning resolutions that are 25% lower than printer resolution. If this is the case, multiplying the result of the scanning resolution calculation by 0.75 will result in acceptable image quality, while keeping file sizes at manageable levels.

Scanning Resolution for Continuous-Tone Printers Equation

$$\text{Scanning resolution} =$$

$$\text{Printer resolution} \times \text{Scale factor}$$

Example   The scanning resolution for an original enlarged by 200%,
                                printed on a 300-spot-per-inch continuous-tone inkjet
                                printer, is:

$$\text{Scanning resolution } = 300 \times 2$$

$$= 600 \text{ samples per inch}$$

4   Scanning Resolution for Video/Multimedia

Ultimately, all multimedia projects are destined for a variety of different electronic devices having some form of monitor or screen displaying graphic images that are often enhanced by motion and sound. Some of these electronic devices have proprietary formats and sizes, but the majority are standardized computer monitors or television screens. All of these devices have relatively low image resolutions. Average computer monitors have an approximate resolution of 72 pixels per inch, while some high-resolution monitors may go as high as 96 pixels per inch, which is significantly lower than the 2,540-spi platesetter output used in printing.

High-resolution images often cannot be displayed on computer monitors in their entirety because the total number of pixels in the vertical and horizontal monitor dimensions are fixed (Table 4.4.1). This means that if a monitor has a resolution of 72 pixels per inch, any scan in excess of 72 samples per inch will result in more pixels than are available on the screen if the scanned original image is greater than the maximum viewable size of the screen. Effectively, only part of the image is seen on the viewable screen area, the rest could be displayed only by the computer video memory and through a user interface that provides scrolling capabilities. If the orig-

Table 4.4.1.
Video standards for IBM and IBM-compatible computers.

Standard	Vertical and Horizontal Resolution	Recommended Monitor Size
Video graphics array (VGA)	640×480	14 and 15 in.
Super VGA	800×600	14 and 15 in.
Super VGA	1,024×768	15 and 17 in.
Super VGA	1,280×1,024	17 in.

inal is smaller than the viewable screen area, then scanning resolutions larger than 72 pixels will result in enlarged images.

The following method for determining scanning resolutions for computer monitor output is based on the assumption that the vertical and horizontal dimensions of the original have to fill the viewable screen area of the monitor. Because of the aforementioned fixed number of monitor screen pixels, the calculation for scanning resolution always involves the division of the original's vertical dimension in inches into the monitor's vertical dimension in pixels. This simple calculation is the optimum scanning resolution and effectively distributes the vertical monitor screen pixels in the vertical dimension of the scanned original.

Another matter of concern is the fixed height to width ratio of monitor screens. This is called the aspect ratio and is calculated by dividing the vertical pixel resolution into the horizontal pixel resolution. The majority of IBM and IBM-compatible computers have an aspect ratio of 1.33, the exception being the 1,280×1,024 resolution, which has an aspect ratio of 1.25. If the vertical to horizontal dimension ratio of the original is higher than the screen display's aspect ratio, portions of the horizontal image dimensions won't be displayed. The method for calculating the cropped size in the original's horizontal dimension is determined by dividing the calculated scanning resolution into the monitor's horizontal pixel resolution. For example, a 9.5×15-in. original to be scanned for output (portrait orientation) on a 1,024×768-ppi monitor should have a scanning resolution of 81 ppi (768 ÷ 9.5). The original's horizontal cropped size should be 12.64 in. (1,024 ÷ 81).

Television, as the dominant communications medium in contemporary culture, will probably play a pivotal role in the evolution of multimedia. Multimedia video is a hybrid form of interactive communications that combines the processing power of computers with analog or digital recording devices capable of capturing photorealistic, stereo audio, and 18–30 frames per second nonflickering motion.

When scanning for analog video output, certain differences between computer RGB monitors and NTSC television screen displays must be compensated. Although the aspect ratio of most computer monitors and television screens is the same, images broadcast on television screens extend beyond the physical boundaries of the screen, a phenomenon which

Figure 4.4.1.
Overscan and under-
scan in TV and RGB
screens.

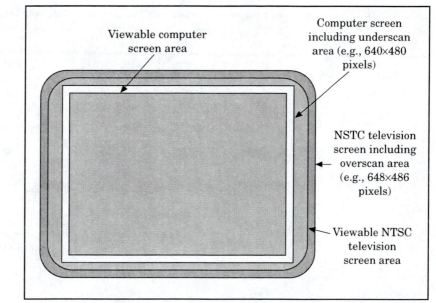

is called overscan; on computer monitors an exact opposite
exists, the underscan scenario (Figure 4.4.1). If not compensated, the scanned image, converted to NTSC video, will have
black borders when displayed on a standard television screen.

The method for calculating optimal scanning resolutions is
essentially the same as for output on RGB computer monitors,
save for the discussed under- and overscan phenomenon,
which must be compensated by increasing the dimensions of
the base image by about 10%.

The pixel shape difference between RGB computer monitors and NTSC television screens has to be addressed as
well. Computer monitor pixels are square, or have a 1:1
ratio, while television screen pixels have a 1:1.17 ratio. If not
compensated by appropriate scaling, scanned images will
appear vertically stretched.

Although scanning resolutions, including compensation
values for NTSC video, can be calculated fairly accurately,
the old adage a "picture is worth a thousand words" gives
rise to the possibility of editing graphics in final output format, either by using NTSC legal filters or NTSC monitors.

**Scanning
Resolution for
Computer
Monitor Output
Equation**

$$\text{Scanning resolution} = \frac{\text{Vertical monitor dimension}}{\text{Vertical dimension of original}}$$

where the vertical monitor dimension is in pixels, and the
vertical dimension of the original is in inches.

Example

An 8×11.5-in. photograph has to fill the title screen of a computer-based multimedia presentation with its 8.5-in. dimension parallel to the vertical monitor dimension. If the computer screen has a resolution of 800×600 pixels, then the scanning resolution and horizontal crop size of the original are:

$$\text{Scanning resolution} = \frac{600}{8}$$

$$= 75 \text{ spi}$$

$$\text{Horizontal crop size} = \frac{800}{75}$$

$$= 10.66 \text{ in.}$$

Scanning Resolution for NTSC–Television Monitor Output Equation

$$\text{Scanning resolution} = \frac{\text{Vertical video display dimension}}{\text{Vertical dimension of original}}$$

where the vertical video display dimension is in pixels, and the vertical dimension of the original is in inches.

Example

A 12.5×17-in. photograph has to fill the title screen of an NTSC television screen multimedia video presentation with its 12.5-in. dimension parallel to the vertical television screen dimension. If the television screen has a resolution of 648×486 pixels, then the scanning resolution and horizontal crop size of the original are:

$$\text{Scanning resolution} = \frac{486}{12.5}$$

$$= 38.88$$

$$\approx 39 \text{ spi}$$

$$\text{Horizontal crop size} = \frac{648}{38.88}$$

$$= 16.66 \text{ in.}$$

5 Scanning Resolution for Line Art

Line art is the term given to originals that have no tonal gradations. Line drawings, black-and-white clipart, text, borders, and frames are examples of line art. In contrast, continuous-tone originals such as photographs have a wide range of tonal gradations and require the halftone process to be reproduced (Figure 4.5.1).

Figure 4.5.1. Reproductions of continuous tones and line art.

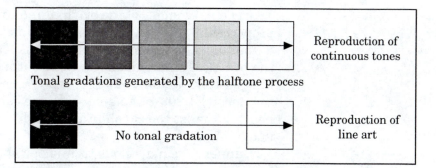

Because tonal gradations are not an issue in the reproduction of line art, the focus shifts to the attainment of straight edges bounding the limits of image elements. Because in digital imaging processes the image areas are made up of a multitude of spots, the potential for pixelized or jagged edges (jaggies) exists. The smaller these spots are, the less visible they turn out to be, which is the reason relatively high output device resolutions must be used when imaging line art.

It follows that scanning resolutions must also be high, but never higher than the highest possible resolution of an output device. For example, a 600-sample-per-inch scan does not yield a better image quality than a 300-sample-per-inch scan if both are printed on a 300-dpi laser printer.

In the commercial printing industry, the output devices of choice are imagesetters and platesetters featuring resolutions in excess of 2,540 spots per inch. The industry standard for line art output is about 1,200 spots per inch, beyond which no noticeable image quality improvements are achieved. A scanning resolution of 800 spi is the minimum resolution at which line art should be scanned and output on imagesetters. Levels below that cause increasingly pronounced pixelized image edges (Figure 4.5.2).

Figure 4.5.2.
Line art scanned at five resolutions.

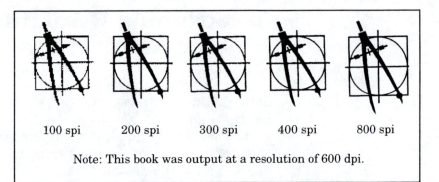

| 100 spi | 200 spi | 300 spi | 400 spi | 800 spi |

Note: This book was output at a resolution of 600 dpi.

Any enlargement of the original requires an equal and proportional increase of scanned samples. There is, however, a limit as to how much enlargement is feasible. For example, the practical enlargement limit for output on 2,540-spi imagesetters would be 200%. At 200% enlargement, doubling the normal 1,200-sample-per-inch scanning resolution would nearly exhaust the capabilities of high-performance 2,540-spi imagesetters.

Scanners are marvelous technological devices and indispensable in the image preparation workflow, but given the option of using scanned line art or line art drawn in vector-based programs (such as Adobe Illustrator), the latter method, though more labor-intensive, is preferable.

The reason is related to the way scanners capture images dot by dot, producing a bitmap, which can't be resized after scanning without image degradation. Vector graphics, on the other hand, are described according to the graphics' outline in a programming language called PostScript. This produces crisper image outlines and smaller file sizes and, most importantly, it provides scalability without negative effects to image quality.

Poor line quality such as faint lines often turn out without any image content at all because, in the line art mode, the scanner evaluates each sample for its level of darkness. If the darkness level of the sample is less than the 50% threshold value, the scanner records it as white, while darkness levels of 50% and more are recorded as image. Thus, good scanning results are predicated by the original line art consisting of dense and uniformly dark lines.

Line Art Scanning Resolution Equation

Scanning resolution = HODR × Scale factor

where *HODR* is the highest output device resolution, but not higher than 1,200. For example, if the highest output device resolution is 2,540 dpi, use 1,200 dpi in the equation.

Example

The scanning resolution for a line art original enlarged by 50%, if output on a 2,540-spi imagesetter, is:

$$\text{Scanning resolution} = 1{,}200 \times 1.5$$

$$= 1{,}800 \text{ spi}$$

6   File Size

When graphic images are scanned, the resulting file sizes can become a productivity issue, as file size affects the speed, efficiency, and processing time needed to complete subsequent operations such as image editing, electronic file transfers, Web page image loading, and output on imagesetters or platesetters, digital printing devices, and proofing devices. Creating larger-than-necessary files will have the negative effect of delaying these operations, thus reducing efficiency and profitability.

The factors affecting file sizes are image size, scanning resolution, bit depth, and color mode.

Of these, image size is the most easily explained. In the case of bitmapped images, the number of bits, the smallest unit that a computer can count and store, changes in direct proportion to changes in image square area. This means that a 4×4-in. image area, by virtue of having a square area of 16 sq. in., will have a file size that is 16 times greater than an image area measuring 1×1 in. or 1 sq. in. Effectively, a scanner's CCD array has to sense a number of fixed samples per unit area that varies according and in direct proportion to the image square area.

Scanning resolution affects file sizes because different scanning resolutions change the number of samples recorded by the scanner's CCD array against an adjustable scale, such as 300 samples per inch. If the scanning resolution is adjusted to 400 instead of 300 samples per inch, more samples are packed into the same unit area, thus increasing the number of samples that are sensed. Since scanning resolution is a two-dimensional phenomenon of a number of samples in horizontal rows and vertical columns, file size is determined by calculating the square of the resolution. Moreover, since scanning resolution affects the entire image area, the image square area must be multiplied by the square of the resolution to determine the number of samples sensed in the entire graphic image.

Each sample sensed by the scanner's CCD array is stored in the computer as a series of ones and zeros. These ones and zeros are representative of the two states in the computer's electronic circuitry, which can be either on or off. A one and a zero usually signify image and nonimage area, respectively. The one and zero are referred to as bits (binary digits), and the order of their sequence is the numeric equivalent of a particular tonal value.

A bitmap is a composite of all bits in an image and defines where output devices such as imagesetters, platesetters, laser printers, or digital proofing machines deposit an image element.

If a scanned sample contains one bit of information, it can be defined as either black or white. Therefore, the one-bit scanning mode is suitable only for line art. Typical examples of line art are line drawings, black-and-white clipart, text, borders, and frames, all of which have only two tonal gradations, image area and nonimage area. (For further information on line art, refer to section 5.)

Originals, such as photographs, have a great many more than two tonal gradations and therefore cannot be reproduced adequately in the line art mode. This is because the one bit per sample used in the line art scan mode will record the image as either image or nonimage area, resulting in a photograph being reproduced in two tones, dropping all other tones. This lack of gray levels in the reproduction of continuous-tone originals is called posterization and can create interesting effects but, if unintended, is obviously not suitable to reproduce the multiple gray levels of continuous-tone originals.

Increasing the bits per sample scanned to more than one bit is called an increase of bit depth. As the bit depth per sample scanned is increased, the number of gray levels that can be reproduced increases exponentially. This is to say, two bits per scanned sample increases the two base tonal gradations of one-bit scanning by a power of two, or four gray levels (2^2). Likewise, four and eight bits per sample scanned would increase the number of possible gray levels to 16 (2^4) and 256 (2^8), respectively. Figure 4.6.1 shows five gray levels out of the 256 that are possible in the eight-bit scanning mode, as well as their respective rank, screen percentages, and binary numbers.

Figure 4.6.1.
Eight-bit gray levels.

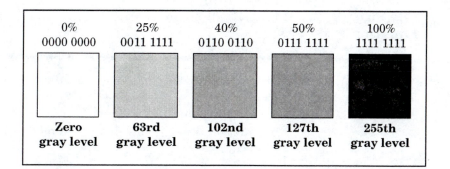

The 256 tonal gradations that eight-bit scanning generates are more than adequate and, in fact, many experts consider gray levels of 100 or less to be satisfactory for the reproduction of continuous-tone originals.

The concept of bit depth can be extended to different color modes such as RGB and CMYK. In each of these color modes, a scanner is actually capturing each color on separate channels as eight-bit (or more) grayscale data. Assuming a scanner can record eight bits per channel, the number of bits for the RGB scanning mode will be 24 per sample (3×8); for the CMYK scanning mode, the number of bits per sample will be 32 (4×8).

The total number of bits in bitmap files with bit depths of more than one bit per sample is thus calculated by multiplying the bit depth with the earlier determined product of the original's square area and the square of the scanning resolution.

Bit depth affects file size in arithmetic progression, which means 32-bit scanning creates file sizes that are four times larger than eight-bit scanning. Since, in computer terminology, we speak of eight contiguous bits as a byte, this becomes the basic unit of measurement for computer storage.

Because bitmap file sizes are usually specified in kilobytes and there are 8,192 bits in a kilobyte, dividing the total number of bits by 8,192 gives the size of bitmaps in kilobytes.

The file format in which scanned image files are saved could change the file size significantly. The mathematical method discussed here is accurate only for image files saved in bitmap (BMP) and uncompressed TIFF formats. Other file formats such as EPS could yield larger file sizes because they include overhead data such as preview image information. Smaller file sizes can be expected when binary-encoded bitmaps are used instead of ASCII encoding. Built-in compression algorithms in file formats such as compressed TIFF, JPEG, and GIF also reduce file sizes significantly.

File Size Equation

File size in kilobytes =

$$\frac{\text{Width} \times \text{Height} \times \text{Resolution}^2 \times \text{Bits per sample}}{8{,}192}$$

Example 1

If a 4×4-in. image is scanned at a resolution of 300 samples per inch in an eight-bit grayscale mode, then the resulting file size is:

$$\text{File size in kilobytes} = \frac{4 \times 4 \times 300^2 \times 8}{8{,}192}$$

$$= \frac{4 \times 4 \times 90{,}000 \times 8}{8{,}192}$$

$$= \frac{11{,}520{,}000}{8{,}192}$$

$$= 1{,}406.25$$

$$\approx 1{,}406$$

Example 2

If the scanning resolution in example 1 is changed to 600 spi, then the file size is:

$$\text{File size in kilobytes} = \frac{4 \times 4 \times 600^2 \times 8}{8{,}192}$$

$$= \frac{4 \times 4 \times 360{,}000 \times 8}{8{,}192}$$

$$= \frac{46{,}080{,}000}{8{,}192}$$

$$= 5{,}625$$

All other variables being equal, doubling the scanning resolution quadruples the file size.

Example 3

If the color mode in example 1 is changed to RGB, then the file size is:

$$\text{File size in kilobytes} = \frac{4 \times 4 \times 300^2 \times 24}{8,192}$$

$$= \frac{4 \times 4 \times 90,000 \times 24}{8,192}$$

$$= \frac{34,560,000}{8,192}$$

$$= 4,218.75$$

$$\approx 4,219$$

All other variables being equal, changing the scanning mode from eight-bit grayscale to RGB triples the file size.

7 Halftone Screen Frequency and Output Resolution

It is an inescapable fact that the number of gray levels digitally generated halftone dots can produce is governed by the size of individual output device spots and by the size of the halftone cell itself. (For further information on halftone and halftone cells, refer to section 1.) The smaller an output device's spots are, the more gray levels it can produce; and the larger the halftone cells are, the more gray levels that are possible. These inverse relationships of size to gray levels are predicated by the simple notion that more dots per unit area will produce more gray levels. There are only two possible ways to produce more dots per unit area: either by reducing the output device spot size (Figure 4.7.1), or enlarging the halftone cell size, which really means that a coarser halftone screen frequency is used (Figure 4.7.2).

The limit as to the number gray levels the human eye is able to distinguish as distinct tonal gradations is thought to be approximately 100, which is well within the capabilities of PostScript levels 1 and 2, both of which can build 256 halftone

Figure 4.7.1.
Increasing gray levels from 64 *(left)* to 256 *(right)* by decreasing output device spot size, while halftone screen frequency remains constant.

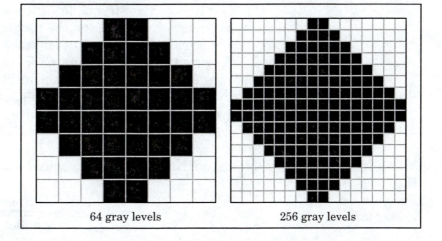

64 gray levels   256 gray levels

Figure 4.7.2.
Increasing gray levels from 64 *(left)* to 256 *(right)* by using a coarser halftone screen frequency while output device spot size remains constant.

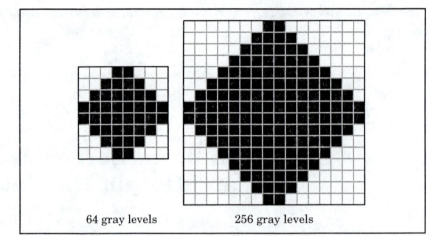

64 gray levels   256 gray levels

dot sizes. The cell size, or number of spots per linear length of a halftone cell that is required to achieve this or any other number of gray levels, is always the square root of the gray levels. Thus, to achieve the 256 gray levels that PostScript supports, a halftone cell must have 16 spots in its linear length ($\sqrt{256}$).

The output resolution, being a fixed quantity in both linear directions, must subsequently be divided by the number of spots in the linear length of the halftone cell to determine the maximum halftone screen frequency required to achieve a given number of gray levels. Therefore, given that imagesetter output resolution is 1,200 spi, 256 gray levels can only be produced with a halftone screen frequency that does not exceed 75 lpi (1,200 ÷ 16). Using a halftone screen frequency higher than 75 lpi would result in fewer than 256 gray levels. Figure 4.7.3 shows the correlation of gray levels to halftone screen frequencies for four output device resolutions.

If the halftone screen frequency is known, or a given screen frequency is desired and the required output resolution has to be calculated, then the mathematical procedure is modified by multiplying the square root of the number of possible or desired gray levels by the halftone screen frequency. For example, 256 gray levels, using an 80 lpi halftone screen frequency, would require an output resolution of 1,280 spi ($\sqrt{256} \times 80$).

Maximum Halftone Screen Frequency Equation

Maximum halftone screen frequency =

$$\frac{\text{Output resolution}}{\sqrt{\text{Number of gray levels}}}$$

Figure 4.7.3.
Gray levels vs.
halftone screen
frequency.

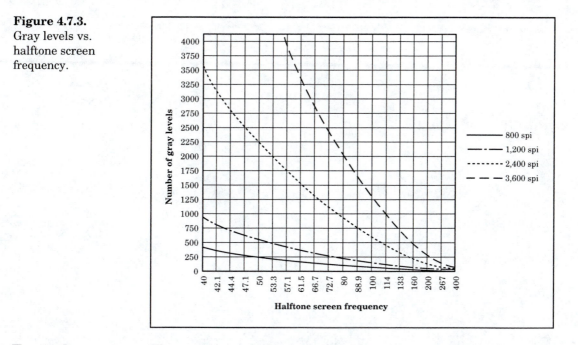

Example

The maximum halftone screen frequency to achieve 256 gray levels on an 800-spi output device is:

$$\text{Maximum halftone screen frequency} = \frac{800}{\sqrt{256}}$$

$$= \frac{800}{16}$$

$$= 50 \text{ lpi}$$

Required Output Resolution Equation

Required output resolution =

$$\text{Halftone lpi} \times \sqrt{\text{Number of gray levels}}$$

Example

The output device resolution required to achieve 256 gray levels using a 133-lpi halftone screen is:

$$\text{Required output resolution} = 133 \times \sqrt{256}$$

$$= 133 \times 16$$

$$= 2,128 \text{ spi}$$

The results can be verified in Figure 4.7.3.

8   Gradient Fill Steps

Background tints with progressively changing tonal values can be produced in most drawing and page layout programs (Figure 4.8.1). There is no general agreement as to what this technique should be called and terms such as vignette, fountain, blend, degradé, or gradient fill all refer to the same technique. For a gradient fill to achieve its desired visual effect, the transition from dark to light tones must be smooth so as to avoid a problem called banding, which is exemplified by visible tonal steps.

Figure 4.8.1.
Gradient fill.

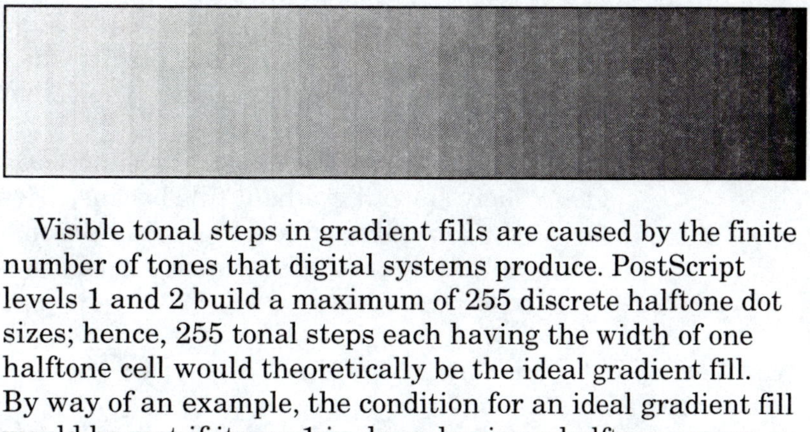

Visible tonal steps in gradient fills are caused by the finite number of tones that digital systems produce. PostScript levels 1 and 2 build a maximum of 255 discrete halftone dot sizes; hence, 255 tonal steps each having the width of one halftone cell would theoretically be the ideal gradient fill. By way of an example, the condition for an ideal gradient fill would be met if it was 1 in. long, having a halftone screen frequency of 150 lpi, and an output resolution of 2,400 spi:

$$\left(\frac{2,400}{150}\right)^2 = 256$$

(For more information on this equation, refer to section 1.)
Given these conditions, a gradient fill longer than 1 in. would necessarily require steps that are longer than the width of one halftone cell, and a great many more halftone

cells per step would be needed if the gradient fill was substantially longer than 1 in. The resulting steps could have noticeably distinct tonal values because of the relatively large area they occupy. Long gradient fills are therefore problematic, especially if the number of steps is substantially reduced due to the use of high halftone screen frequencies or coarse output device resolutions, factors that individually and in combination with each other will reduce the number of possible tonal steps.

The aforementioned equation works for gradient fills that extend over the full tonal range from 0 to 100%, but for gradient fills with shorter tonal ranges it has to be slightly modified. For example, if a gradient fill starts at a 30% and ends at an 80% tonal value, then the available steps are reduced by the difference between the starting and ending tonal percentage values, or by 50% in this example. The 2,400-spi output and 150-lpi halftone screen frequency example referred to earlier would therefore be reduced from 255 to 127 steps (255×0.5).

In addition to this mathematical approach to gradient fills, there is a technical solution to the problem of banding that works with bitmapped images as opposed to the PostScript-generated ones. It is called "noise" and involves the introduction of extraneous pixels, which has the effect of blurring the tonal interfaces, thus creating smoother gradient fills.

Finally, PostScript 3 has the potential of creating exceedingly smooth gradient fills because of the 4,096 gray levels it supports. If used together with extremely high resolution output devices, gradient fills with 500 or more steps are a real possibility.

Number of Gradient Fill Steps Equation

Number of gradient fill steps =

$$\left(\frac{\text{Output resolution}}{\text{Halftone screen frequency}} \right)^2 \times \left(\frac{\text{Maximum} - \text{Minimum}}{100} \right)$$

where *minimum* and *maximum* are the starting and ending tonal percentages of a gradient fill, respectively.

Example

A gradient fill with starting and ending tonal percentages of 20% and 80%, respectively, when reproduced with a 150-lpi halftone screen frequency and imaged on an imagesetter having a resolution of 1,200 spi, requires a number of steps that are no less than:

$$\text{Number of gradient fill steps} = \left(\frac{1,200}{150}\right)^2 \times \left(\frac{80-20}{100}\right)$$

$$= 8^2 \times \left(\frac{60}{100}\right)$$

$$= 8^2 \times 0.6$$

$$= 64 \times 0.6$$

$$= 38.4$$

$$\approx 38$$

9 Halftone Dot Size

Current high-performance drum-based imagesetters or plate-setters can generate image spots as small as 5 µm, which is equivalent to 5 millionths of a meter.

These extremely small spots, of which halftone dots are made up, contribute in large part to the high-fidelity reproductions possible with digital imaging systems, but this diminutiveness can also cause very fine image elements, such as fine lines pointing to halftone image details, to be discontinuous or broken.

The physical limit, as to the smallest possible image element that can be reproduced, is governed mainly by the coarseness or resolution of printing plates and the type of substrate used in printing.

Good conventional printing plates just about match the resolution of imagesetters and platesetters, as their grain size is also about 5 µm.

Because of the enormous number of existing types and grades of paper, it is difficult to make generalizations about papers' ability to hold extremely fine detail. A 2% dot or a 0.3-pt. hairline is probably near the lower limit of reproducibility for premium-coated papers, while for some very porous, uncoated, and newsprint papers, the lower limit of fine image detail reproducibility may be 12% dot sizes or a 0.75-pt. hairline.

Halftone dot percentages alone, however, are not valid indicators of dot size; at a given halftone screen percentage, high-frequency halftone screens produce significantly smaller dot sizes than low-frequency halftone screens.

Consider the coarse and fine halftone cells shown in Figure 4.9.1, both of which were imaged with identical output resolutions. The fine halftone cell can accommodate

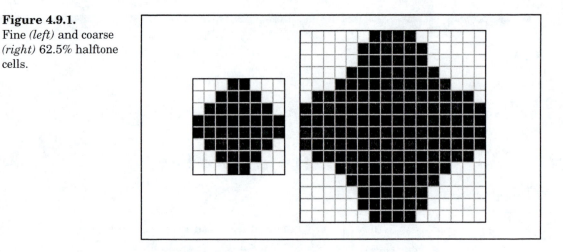

64 spots, 40 of which are turned into image spots ($^{40}\!/_{64} \times 100 =$ 62.5%), while the coarse halftone cell can accommodate 256 spots, 160 of which are turned into image areas ($^{160}\!/_{256} \times 100 =$ 62.5%). Therefore, both halftone cells represent 62.5% halftone screen percentages, but the coarse halftone cell is exactly twice as large and fits twice as many spots in the vertical and horizontal dimensions as the fine halftone cell. If the coarse and fine halftone cells represent 100 and 200 lpi, respectively, it follows that doubling halftone screen frequencies cuts in half the linear height and width of halftone dots.

Calculating the size of a 100%, 200-lpi halftone dot is a simple matter of dividing 1 in. by the halftone screen frequency, or $1 \div 200 = 0.005$ in. But if halftone cell sizes of less than 100% have to be calculated, the halftone cell area must be proportionally reduced. Mathematically, this is done by calculating the square root of the halftone screen percentage, the result of which is then divided by 10 times the halftone screen frequency.

Halftone Dot Size Equation

$$\text{Halftone dot size} = \frac{\sqrt{\text{Halftone screen percentage}}}{10 \times \text{Halftone screen frequency}}$$

Example

If a particular uncoated paper can usually hold 6% highlight dots at a halftone screen frequency of 100 lpi, then the size of this 6% dot is:

$$\text{Halftone dot size in inches} = \frac{\sqrt{6}}{10 \times 100}$$

$$= \frac{2.4494897}{1,000}$$

$$= 0.002449489 \text{ in.}$$

$$\text{Halftone dot size (in } \mu m) = 0.002449489 \times 25,400$$

$$= 62.2$$

$$\text{Halftone dot size (in points)} = 0.002449489 \times 72.30658$$

$$= 0.17711$$

If this paper is known to reproduce hairline elements satis-factorily only up to a thinness of 0.5 pt., then the halftone screen frequency has to be reduced 2.9 times (0.5 ÷ 0.17711) from 100 to 35 lpi.

10   Unsharp Masking

Continuous-tone images scanned for print reproduction must almost always undergo a depth and contrast enhancing process called unsharp masking. The need for contrast enhancement arises from the technical limitations of the scanning and printing processes.

On the scanning side, a lack of contrast between adjacent tones is in part caused by a scanner's limited sensitivity to shadow details. In addition, the limitations imposed by digital computers result in scanned samples that happen to fall directly on the interface between light and dark tones to be averaged, thus reducing tonal contrast even more.

For images destined to be printed, the obligatory halftone process tends to reduce definition between adjacent tonal values because the number of gray levels available to accentuate tonal differences is greatly reduced, especially when high-frequency halftone screens are used.

During printing, ink is applied to paper using pressure. This causes adjacent tones to be less distinguishable from each other due to a phenomenon called dot gain. (For further information on dot gain, refer to part 2, section 1.)

Sharpening is a process that accentuates the very edges of adjacent tones, thus better delineating image details and along with it providing the optical illusion of improved image contrast. Sharpening can be performed during scanning or as a post-scanning process in image-editing programs such as Photoshop.

Image-editing programs usually have several sharpening options ranging from simple sharpening filters to more complex unsharp masking functions. Unsharp masking is usually the preferred tool because, unlike simple masking filters, it accentuates only the periphery of adjacent tones without emphasizing tonal areas beyond, including undesirable specks caused by noise.

The extent to which sharpening can be tolerated without causing unnatural-looking halos framing image elements depends on the scanning resolution and image content.

The relationship between scanning resolution and allowable sharpening levels is approximately linear, in that, for every doubling of scanning resolution, sharpening levels can also be doubled. Higher output resolutions can also tolerate greater sharpening levels.

The sharpening criteria dictated by image content are more subjective, but in general long shots and images with an abundance of detail can tolerate more sharpening than close-up shots with subtle tonal transitions such as human faces.

It is possible to apply sharpening to select portions of an image, which permits, for example, selective sharpening of facial features such as the eyes.

The mathematical method and recommended values for various sharpening settings that follow are specifically relevant for Photoshop. Other image-editing programs have sharpening tools that may be dissimilar in details and terminology, but not in fundamental principles and applications.

Photoshop allows sharpening levels to be controlled by means of three adjustable settings called radius, amount, and threshold.

Radius is the most critical setting and should be adjusted first. It controls the spatial width that is affected by the sharpening process. High and low radius settings signify wide and narrow zonal sharpening fringes, respectively. A given sharpening value signifies the width in scanning samples of two adjacent tones. Effectively this means a radius setting of 1.0 creates a two-sample-wide zone that extends equally into the adjacent light and dark tones. The width of this zone is calculated by dividing the scanning resolution by 200. For example, an image scanned at a resolution of 400 spi should have a radius setting of 2.0 (400 ÷ 200; Figure 4.10.1). Within this zone the darker tone is made even darker and the lighter tone even lighter.

The term "amount" aptly denotes the magnitude of tonal density increase in the darker tone and decrease in the lighter tone. There is no mathematical method to determine amount values, but empirical data seems to suggest amount values of 200% as a good starting point (Figure 4.10.1). High

Figure 4.10.1.
Unsharp masking
not applied and
applied at two
radius settings.

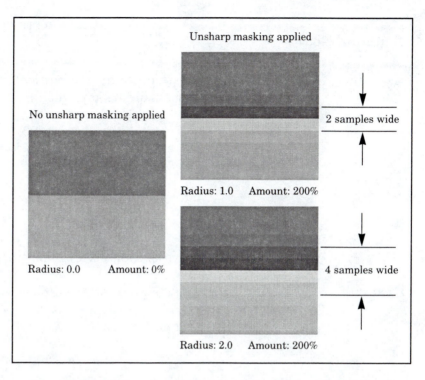

and low values mean large and small tonal density changes, respectively.

The threshold setting adjusts the sensitivity required for sharpening to occur. High threshold values require greater tonal differences between adjacent tones for the sharpening process to be activated than low threshold values. Consequently, high threshold values result in less sharpening than low threshold values. As for amount settings, no mathematical method is used to determine threshold settings. Threshold values of 3 or 4 seem to yield the best results for most reproductions. Threshold values of 10 and above are not suitable to detect a majority of tonal interface differences and as such result in inadequately sharpened reproductions.

The radius values discussed thus far are based on the assumption of a normal viewing distance of about 11–13 in.

Images such as large posters or billboards, which are typically viewed from greater distances, can tolerate larger radius values. An alternate equation that takes the viewing distance into consideration is useful for images that are viewed from distances longer than for normal reading materials such as books. This equation requires the multiplication of scanning resolution by the viewing distance and a constant factor of 0.0004.

Radius Equation No. 1

$$\text{Radius} = \frac{\text{Scanning resolution}}{200}$$

Example

If an image is scanned at a resolution of 300 spi, then the radius setting should be adjusted to:

$$\text{Radius} = \frac{300}{200}$$

$$= 1.5$$

Radius Equation No. 2

$$\text{Radius} =$$

$$\text{Scanning resolution} \times \text{Viewing distance in inches} \times 0.0004$$

Example

If the viewing distance for an outdoor poster is estimated at 36 in., then an image scanned at 200 spi should have a radius setting of:

$$\text{Radius} = 200 \times 36 \times 0.0004$$

$$= 2.88$$

11 Scaling for Enlargement or Reduction

At the pre-publishing stage, designers are often faced with the problem of having to position artwork, photographs, or other image elements in a designated area on a page layout that is either smaller or larger than the original image's size.

A specific case in point would be an image measuring 40×50 picas that has to fit a 20-pica-wide column. If the 40-pica dimension has to be reduced to 20 picas, the proportional reduced 50-pica dimension is found by first dividing the desired 20-pica dimension by the original's equivalent dimension, i.e., $20 \div 40 = 0.5$. Then, by multiplying this result by the 50-pica dimension, i.e., $50 \times 0.5 = 25$, the proportionally reduced 50-pica dimension is found. Conversely, if the 50-pica dimension had to be reduced to 20 picas, the proportionally reduced 40-pica dimension is found by again dividing the desired 20-pica dimension by the original's equivalent dimension, which in this case is 50 picas, i.e., $20 \div 50 = 0.4$. As before, the result is then multiplied by the dimension that has to be proportionally reduced, i.e., $0.4 \times 40 = 16$. Note that the first calculation results in an upright or portrait image orientation, while the second calculation produces an oblong or landscape image orientation.

An alternate drafting procedure, called the diagonal line method, will produce an identical, albeit graphic, result.

For this method, a rectangle having the original's dimensions and a diagonal line connecting the lower left and upper right corners is drawn. If the method is used for proportional enlargements, the vertical line, lower horizontal baseline, and left vertical line are extended an indefinite distance.

The new desired size, whether a vertical or horizontal dimension, is measured on the respective left vertical or horizontal baseline. From this point a line running parallel to the horizontal baseline or left vertical line is drawn until it

Figure 4.11.1.
Diagonal line method of scaling for reductions or enlargements.

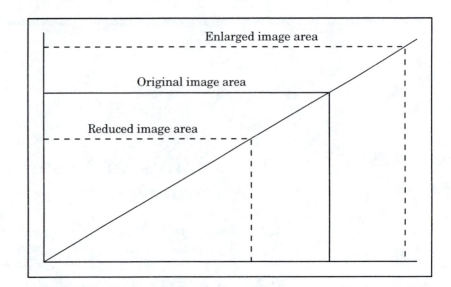

meets the diagonal line, where it is projected perpendicularly to form the new proportionally reduced or enlarged image area (Figure 4.11.1).

When scanned images are scaled, the image resolution changes in direct proportion to the enlargement or reduction. That is, if a scanned image is placed on a page and is scaled to 200%, the image resolution is decreased by a factor of two, and when the image is scaled to 50%, the image resolution is increased by a factor of two (Figure 4.11.2). Therefore, when calculating scanning resolutions for images that have to be reproduced at sizes other than 100%, a scale factor is used to obtain the intended resolution.

The scale factor is calculated by dividing the desired output dimension by the equivalent original dimension. If, for example, the shorter side of an 8×10-in. original has to be enlarged to 12 in., the scale factor is 1.5 (12 ÷ 8).

**Scaled
Dimension
Equation**

Scaled dimension =

$$\frac{\text{Desired dimension} \times \text{Original dimension to be scaled}}{\text{Original dimension equivalent to desired dimension}}$$

Example

If an 8×10 in. original has to fit a 3.5-in.-wide column with its 8-in. dimension, then the original's proportionally reduced 10-in. dimension is:

$$\text{Scaled dimension} = \frac{3.5 \times 10}{8}$$

Figure 4.11.2.
Resolutions of
scanned image before
and after scaling it
at 50% and 200%.

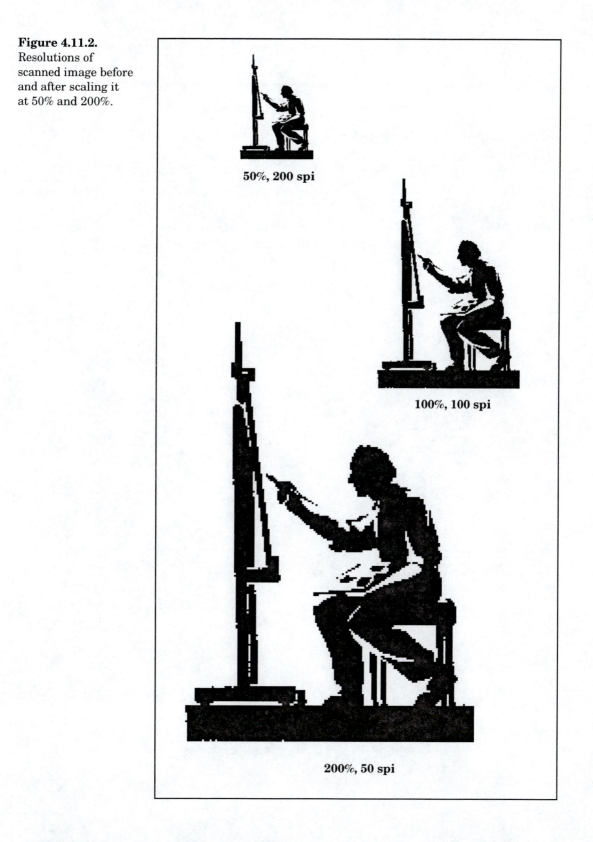

50%, 200 spi

100%, 100 spi

200%, 50 spi

$$= \frac{35}{8}$$

$$= 4.375 \text{ in.}$$

Scale Factor Equation

Scale factor =

$$\frac{\text{Output dimension}}{\text{Original dimension equivalent to output dimension}}$$

Example

If the 7.5-in. dimension of an 4.5×7.5-in. original has to be output at 11.25 in., then the scale factor is:

$$\text{Scale factor } = \frac{11.25}{7.5}$$

$$= 1.5$$

12 Telecommunication Transfer Speeds

During the last decade or so, the transmission of data by electronic carrier technology has become so commonplace that even children don't think twice to send or receive email, communicate via Internet chat lines, or print out pictures received from distant continents. We live in an increasingly "wired" world in which physical distance has become almost irrelevant with regard to sending or receiving data across the country or across the world.

More than most industries, the printing industry has benefited from this technological revolution, because it is now possible to send or receive nearly instantly its core product—visual content—via carrier technologies such as Ethernet in a local area network (LAN) within an organization, or via the airwaves through satellite transmission.

It is now almost the rule rather than the exception that service bureaus and prepress houses accept data electronically. Reporters file their reports and digital pictures via satellite transmission to their editors, and editorial departments then dispatch data electronically to several remote locations where a publication can then be printed simultaneously in different parts of the country.

Telecommunication requirements for the graphic communications industry are demanding, because the graphic images, including color information, that are typically processed tend to be quite data intensive. Until recently it could take hours to transmit image information electronically. For example, an 8×10-in. image scanned in the CMYK mode at 300 spi has a file size of 28,125 kilobytes (for further information on file sizes, refer to section 6); to transfer this image on a 1,200 bits per second (bps) modem would have required 65 hours.

Transmission speeds have increased by many orders of magnitude, making electronic transfers even more feasible for the printing industry. Here again by way of an example, the aforementioned CMYK image would take today only three minutes if it were transmitted on a T-1 carrier at a rated transmission speed of 1.544 megabits per second (Mbps).

The remainder of this section will deal with the mathematical method to calculate electronic transmission speeds. It must be said, however, that because of the plethora of carrier technologies, each one having its own technical specification (Table 4.12.1), any transmission speed result derived from a single equation will fall short of an exact result and the mathematical method discussed here must be understood as a rule-of-thumb method to determine approximate transmission speeds.

Several assumptions will be made to simplify the equations and render them useful for all carrier technologies. First it will be assumed that there are 8 bits to a byte, which is almost always true these days. Furthermore, a couple of extra bits or 20% will be added to the variable that converts bytes to bits (the numeric value 10 in the equation), which represents the overhead of the communication. This is quite typical for modem communication, such as for telephone connections. A modem typically transmits a byte as 10 bits: 8 bits data, plus a start bit and a stop bit.

The same approach will be taken for all other transmission technologies and their respective protocols, because they also require overhead control data beyond the data to be transferred, though their actual overhead percentages may vary somewhat from the 20% value assigned in the equation.

The results that the equation yields must be considered "best case" transmission speeds, because shared transmission technologies like Ethernet, T-1, or frame relay will actually be considerably less, as the data may have to wait for other data in the network. For example, in Ethernet data transmission, delays are caused by collisions of data packets and recovery time.

Furthermore, the predominant definitions of kilobytes and megabytes of 1,000 bytes and 1,000,000 bytes, respectively, are used in the equation. There is no general agreement in the computer field, as some manufacturers and standards continue to specify the historical usage of kilobytes and megabytes to mean 1,024 bytes (2^{10}), and 1,048,576 bytes

Table 4.12.1.
Various transmission methods.

Transmission Method	Transmission Speed	Transmission Media	Typical Environments
Telephone service	Up to 56 Kbps	Twisted pair (TP)	Home, small business
Integrated services digital networks (ISDN)	Basic rate interface: 64 Kbps–128 Kbps Primary rate interface: 1.544 Mbps	TP T-1 line	Home, small business Medium and large enterprise access
Satellite	400 Kbps	Airwaves	Print, broadcast media, telephone companies
Special mission satellite	2.56 Mbps	Airwaves	Meteorology
Frame relay	56 Kbps–1.544 Mbps	TP or coaxial cable (CC)	Large company backbone for LANs to ISP, ISP to Internet infrastructure
T-1	1.544 Mbps	TP, CC, or optical fiber (OF)	Large company to ISP, ISP to Internet infrastructure
Digital subscriber line (DSL)	512 Kbps–8 Mbps	TP used as a digital broadband medium	Home, small business, enterprise access using copper lines
Cable modem	512 Kbps–52 Mbps; 52 Mbps is subdivided among individual users	CC (usually uses Ethernet); sometimes telephone used for upstream requests	Home, business, school access
Ethernet	10 Mbps	10Base-T (TP); 10Base-2 or -5 (CC); 10Base-F (OF)	Business local area network (LAN)
T-3	44.736 Mbps	CC	ISP to Internet infrastructure; smaller links within Internet infrastructure
Fast Ethernet	100 Mbps	100Base-T4 (TP); 100Base-TX (TP); 100Base-FX (OF)	Workstations with 10-Mbps Ethernet cards plug into a fast Ethernet LAN
Fiber distributed data interface (FDDI)	100 Mbps	OF	Large, wide range LAN usually in a large company or a larger ISP
Asynchronous transfer mode (ATM)	25–622 Mbps	Independent of physical bearer format	Network backbone for large organizations such as news services, universities

megabytes to mean 1,024 bytes (2^{10}), and 1,048,576 bytes (2^{20}), respectively, while others use the previous definition.

Finally, the transmission time between two points is limited by the slowest component between them. For example, if transferring a file from a floppy disk over a high-speed LAN to another computer, the limiting factor is how fast the computer can read the data from a secondary storage medium. Typical values might be a transfer rate of 10 megabits/sec. for Ethernet and 0.125 megabytes/sec. for a peak transfer rate from a floppy. Thus, in theory, the Ethernet is eight times faster than the computer can read the data from a floppy disk.

Since there is no possible way to predict any of these factors, the transmission speeds calculated by the equation used must be considered good approximations, which in most cases are probably somewhat faster than what is achievable.

Transmission Speed Equations*   If file size is in kilobytes and transmission speed is in kilobits per second, the transmission time in seconds is calculated by:

$$\frac{\text{File size in kilobytes} \times 10}{\text{Transmission speed in kilobits per second}}$$

If file size is in megabytes and transmission speed is in kilobits per second, transmission time in seconds is calculated by:

$$\frac{\text{File size in megabytes} \times 10}{\text{Transmission speed in megabits per second}}$$

If file size is in kilobytes and transmission speed is in megabits per second, transmission time in seconds is calculated by:

$$\frac{\text{File size in kilobytes} \times 10}{1,000 \times \text{Transmission speed in megabits per second}}$$

If file size is in megabytes and transmission speed is in kilobits per second, transmission time in seconds is calculated by:

---

*File sizes are almost always expressed in kilobytes or megabytes and transmission speeds in kilobits/sec. or megabits/sec.

$$\frac{1{,}000 \times \text{File size in megabytes} \times 10}{\text{Transmission speed in kilobits per second}}$$

Example 1

A color photograph measuring 8.5×11 in., when scanned in CMYK mode at 300 spi, will have a file size of 33,699 kilobytes. If this file is transmitted via ISDN at a rated speed of 128 kilobits per second, the transmission time will be:

$$\text{Transmission time in seconds} = \frac{33{,}699 \times 10}{128}$$

$$= \frac{336{,}990}{128}$$

$$= 2632.734375 \text{ seconds}$$

$$= 43.87 \text{ minutes}$$

$$\approx 44 \text{ minutes}$$

Example 2

A color photograph measuring 8.5×11 in., when scanned in CMYK mode at 300 spi, will have a file size of 33.699 megabytes. If this file is transmitted via ISDN at a rated speed of 0.128 megabits per second, the transmission time will be:

$$\text{Transmission time in seconds} = \frac{33.699 \times 10}{0.128}$$

$$= \frac{336.990}{0.128}$$

$$= 2632.734375 \text{ seconds}$$

$$= 43.87 \text{ minutes}$$

$$\approx 44 \text{ minutes}$$

Example 3

A color photograph measuring 8.5×11 in., when scanned in CMYK mode at 300 spi, will have a file size of 33,699 kilobytes. If this file is transmitted via ISDN at a rated speed of 0.128 megabits per second, the transmission time will be:

$$\text{Transmission time in seconds} = \frac{33{,}699 \times 10}{1{,}000 \times 0.128}$$

$$= \frac{336{,}990}{128}$$

$$= 2632.734375 \text{ seconds}$$

$$= 43.87 \text{ minutes}$$

$$\approx 44 \text{ minutes}$$

Example 4   A color photograph measuring 8.5×11 in., when scanned in CMYK mode at 300 spi, will have a file size of 33.699 megabytes. If this file is transmitted via ISDN at a rated speed of 128 kilobits per second, the transmission time will be:

$$\text{Transmission time in seconds} = \frac{1{,}000 \times 33.699 \times 10}{128}$$

$$= \frac{336{,}990}{128}$$

$$= 2632.734375 \text{ seconds}$$

$$= 43.87 \text{ minutes}$$

$$\approx 44 \text{ minutes}$$

Note: The four preceding examples have the same file sizes and transmission speeds, but are expressed in either kilobytes or megabytes and kilobits/sec. or megabits/sec., respectively. Consequently, all four results are identical.

Part 5
Common Conversions

The graphic communications industry increasingly is competing in a global economy and must therefore be conversant with the systems of measurement used by potential customers in all parts of the world.

Fortunately, the metric system, also known as Systèm International d' Unités, abbreviated SI, is the legal system of weights and measures in most countries of the world.

In the United States, the Metric Conversion Act, passed in 1975, officially encouraged use of the metric system, but because of the voluntary nature of this act, the metric system has not been as widely accepted here as in most other countries of the world. As a result, in the United States customary units such as feet, gallons, and pounds are still the predominant units of measurement.

The conversion from the metric system to customary units and vice versa requires constant factors, which were refined in 1959.

U.S. customary units for the most part have the same relationship to metric units as British or imperial customary units, with the notable exceptions of some volume and capacity units such as pints, quarts, gallons, gills, bushels, and pecks. Weights and measures as defined by British statute may still be used in some countries belonging to the Commonwealth of Nations.

The following three sections give methods of calculation, including the appropriate conversion factors to convert from metric units to customary units and vice versa.

1 Nonmetric to Metric Conversions

Length

Centimeters = Inch × 2.54

Meters = Feet × 0.3048

Centimeters = Feet × 30.48

Millimeters = Inch × 25.4

Meters = Yards × 0.9144

Kilometers = Nautical miles × 1.852

Kilometers = Statute miles × 1.60934

Area

Square millimeters = Square inch × 645.16

Square centimeters = Square inch × 6.4516

Square centimeters = Square feet × 929.0304

Square meters = Square feet × 0.09203

Square meters = Square yards × 0.836123

Square meters = Acres × 4046.8564

Hectares = Acres × 0.4046856

Hectares = Square miles × 258.9988

Square kilometers = Square miles × 2.589988

Power

Watts = Horsepower × 745.7

Kilowatts = Horsepower × 0.7457

Metric horsepower = Horsepower × 1.01387

Pressure

Kilopascals = Pounds/square inch × 6.895

Mass

Milligrams = Grains × 64.79891
Grams = Grains × 0.064799
Grams = Drams × 1.77185
Grams = Ounces × 28.349523
Kilograms = Ounces × 0.0283495
Kilograms = Pounds × 0.4535924
Metric tons = Tons, long × 1.0161
Metric tons = Tons, short × 0.9072
Kilograms = Tons, long × 1016.0469

Volume and Capacity

Cubic centimeters = Cubic inches × 16.387064
Cubic meters = Cubic feet × 0.0283168
Cubic meters = Cubic yards × 0.7646
Liters = Cubic inches × 0.016387
Milliliters = Fluid drams × 3.6966
Liters = Cubic feet × 28.316847
Liters = Fluid ounces (U.S.) × 0.0296
Milliliters = Fluid ounces (U.S.) × 29.5729
Liters = Gallons (imperial) × 4.46
Liters = Gallons (U.S.) × 3.7854
Liters = Pints (imperial) × 0.5683
Liters = Pints (U.S.) × 0.4732
Liters = Quarts (imperial) × 1.1365
Liters = Quarts (U.S.) × 0.9464

2 Metric to Nonmetric Conversions

Length

Inches = Centimeters ÷ 2.54
Feet = Meters ÷ 0.3048
Feet = Centimeters ÷ 30.48
Inches = Millimeters ÷ 25.4
Yards = Meters ÷ 0.9144
Nautical miles = Kilometers ÷ 1.852
Statute miles = Kilometers ÷ 1.609344

Area

Square inches = Square millimeters ÷ 645.16
Square inches = Square centimeters ÷ 6.4516
Square feet = Square centimeters ÷ 929.0304
Square feet = Square meters ÷ 0.09203
Square yards = Square meters ÷ 0.836123
Acres = Square meters ÷ 4046.8564
Acres = Hectares ÷ 0.4046856
Square miles = Hectares ÷ 258.9988
Square miles = Square kilometers ÷ 2.589988

Power

Horsepower = Watts ÷ 745.7
Horsepower = Kilowatts ÷ 0.7457
Horsepower = Metric horsepower ÷ 1.01387

Pressure

Pounds/square inches = Kilopascals ÷ 6.895

Mass

Grains = Milligrams ÷ 64.79891
Grains = Grams ÷ 0.064799
Drams = Grams ÷ 1.77185
Ounces = Grams ÷ 28.349523
Ounces = Kilograms ÷ 0.0283495
Pounds = Kilograms ÷ 0.4535924
Tons, long = Metric tons ÷ 1.0161
Tons, short = Metric tons ÷ 0.9072
Tons, long = Milograms ÷ 1016.0469

Volume and Capacity

Cubic inches = Cubic centimeters ÷ 16.387064
Cubic feet = Cubic meters ÷ 0.0283168
Cubic yards = Cubic meters ÷ 0.7646
Cubic inches = Liters ÷ 0.016387
Fluid drams = Milliliters ÷ 3.6966
Cubic feet = Liters ÷ 28.316847
Fluid ounces (U.S.) = Liters ÷ 0.0296
Fluid ounces (U.S.) = Milliliters ÷ 29.5729
Gallons (imperial) = Liters ÷ 4.46
Gallons (U.S.) = Liters ÷ 3.7854
Pints (imperial) = Liters ÷ 0.5683
Pints (U.S.) = Liters ÷ 0.4732
Quarts (imperial) = Liters ÷ 1.1365
Quarts (U.S.) = Liters ÷ 0.9464

3   Temperature Conversions

Temperature

Degrees Celsius = (Degrees Fahrenheit − 32) × 0.555555

Degrees Fahrenheit = (Degrees Celsius × 1.8) + 32

Installing ABACUS Software

Windows™ 95/98 Installation Instructions

1. Insert the accompanying disk into the appropriate drive in your computer.
2. From the Windows 95/98 desktop, double-click on the "My Computer" icon.
3. Double-click on the icon representing the drive in which the disk has been inserted.
4. Double-click on the icon titled "Setup."
5. The installation program creates a program group named "ABACUS."
6. To run "ABACUS," press the "Start" button and select "Programs." Then choose "ABACUS."

Windows™ 3.1 Installation Instructions

1. Insert the accompanying disk into the appropriate drive in your computer.
2. From File Manager or Program Manager, choose Run from the File Menu.
3. Type <drive>\Aba3.x\SETUP.
4. The installation program creates a Program Manager group named "ABACUS."
5. To run "ABACUS," double-click on the "ABACUS" icon shaped like an abacus.

Index

About the Author

Manfred Breede began his lifelong career in the graphic arts industry by working as an apprentice pressman in Hamburg, Germany, and continued to work in printing production for 12 years in Germany, the Netherlands, Sweden, and Canada.

In 1972, Breede began teaching graphic arts and other technical subjects at the secondary school level in Quebec, Canada. In 1979, he earned his bachelor's degree in education from McGill University, Montreal, Canada.

In addition to teaching high school, Breede was involved in teacher education at McGill University as a part-time member of the faculty of education and served a one-year term as president of the Provincial Association of Graphic Arts Teachers (Quebec).

In 1987 Breede transferred to his present position at Ryerson Polytechnic University in Toronto, Canada, where he is a professor in the School of Graphic Communications Management, teaching printing processes and quality control courses.

Breede is also an industry consultant, specializing in print quality and efficiency, and is a prolific developer of print quality and graphic arts educational software.

About GATF

The Graphic Arts Technical Foundation is a nonprofit, scientific, technical, and educational organization dedicated to the advancement of the graphic communications industries worldwide. Its mission is to serve the field as the leading resource for technical information and services through research and education.

For 75 years the Foundation has developed leading edge technologies and practices for printing. GATF's staff of researchers, educators, and technical specialists partner with nearly 14,000 corporate members in over 80 countries to help them maintain their competitive edge by increasing productivity, print quality, process control, and environmental compliance, and by implementing new techniques and technologies. Through conferences, satellite symposia, workshops, consulting, technical support, laboratory services, and publications, GATF strives to advance a global graphic communications community.

The GATF*Press* publishes books on nearly every aspect of the field; learning modules (step-by-step instruction booklets); audiovisuals (CD-ROMs, videocassettes, slides, and audiocassettes); and research and technology reports. It also publishes *GATFWorld,* a bimonthly magazine of technical articles, industry news, and reviews of specific products.

For more detailed information on GATF products and services, please visit our website *http://www.gatf.org* or write to us at 200 Deer Run Road, Sewickley, PA 15143-2600 (phone: 412/741-6860).

Orders to:
GATF Orders
P.O. Box 1020
Sewickley, PA 15143-1020
Phone (U.S. and Canada only): 800/662-3916
Phone (all other countries): 412/741-5733
Fax: 412/741-0609
Email: gatforders@abdintl.com

GATF*Press:* Selected Titles

Colophon

Handbook of Graphic Arts Equations was produced digitally as an on-demand publication at the Graphic Arts Technical Foundation (GATF). The interior and cover were created on an Apple Macintosh PowerPC using QuarkXPress. Illustrations were created in Adobe Illustrator, Adobe Photoshop, and Macromedia FreeHand. The primary typefaces used for the interior of the book were New Century Schoolbook and Helvetica.

The files for the cover were preflighted and imposed digitally two-up on a 20×28-in. six-color Komori Lithrone 28 sheetfed press with aqueous coater. The cover was printed on Kivar 314 Performa Chrome paper from Rexam DSI.

The QuarkXPress files for the book's interior were output as Adobe PostScript files by printing to disk. The interior of the book was printed on a Xerox DocuTech 6180 using Matrix 20-lb. bond. The preprinted litho covers and the interior of the book were then bound inline to the DocuTech using the Bourg 2000 perfect binder.